Equal Rights Association

The Constitution of Rhode Island and equal rights

Equal Rights Association

The Constitution of Rhode Island and equal rights

ISBN/EAN: 9783337124922

Printed in Europe, USA, Canada, Australia, Japan

Cover: Foto ©Suzi / pixelio.de

More available books at **www.hansebooks.com**

THE

CONSTITUTION OF RHODE ISLAND

AND

EQUAL RIGHTS.

———◦◦⟨◦⟩◦◦———

I have no doubt that an act of the General Assembly inviting the qualified electors of the State, assembled by delegates in a Convention to frame a Constitution, to be submitted to the people of the State for their approval, would be a lawful proceeding. Nor have I any doubt that such a Convention ought to hold.   *ABRAHAM PAYNE.*

———◦◦⟨◦⟩◦◦———

PUBLISHED BY THE

EQUAL RIGHTS ASSOCIATION.

1881.

INDEX.

THE CONSTITUTION OF RHODE ISLAND

AND

EQUAL RIGHTS.

—

This pamphlet is published by the Equal Rights Association, for the purpose of putting into a form convenient for reference, the facts and arguments adduced in the spring of 1881 in favor of a new constitution, and an equal and extended suffrage for Rhode Island.

———

THE QUALIFICATIONS OF ELECTORS IN RHODE ISLAND.

The owner of real estate gets upon the registry of voters by virtue of his real estate.

The native born, owner of personality, pays his taxes of over one dollar, and thus gets upon the registry.

The native who owns no taxable property must register in the year preceding that in which the vote is to be cast, and pay a tax of one dollar, or he cannot vote. At present, and for the past four years, he is required by law to register personally each year, and to pay his tax on or before the second Saturday in January. If registry taxes for one year are not paid, the Constitution forbids the vote until the arrears for two years are paid up. To those who serve in the State militia, the registry tax for such year is remitted.

The foreign-born citizen, although doing military duty, or paying a tax upon personal property, cannot vote unless he owns real estate to the value of $134.

The following article, which appeared in the Boston *Herald* of November 6, 1880, is here inserted, together with a brief *addendum* by the same writer, DR. L. F. C. GARVIN:

To the Editor of the Herald:—As our little State, with its something more than 250,000 inhabitants, is the only one of the 38 in which a popular government does not exist, a succinct statement of our condition may be interesting to some of your readers without, as well as to the many within, the borders of Rhode Island. The best way to understand our present status is to glance briefly at the successive steps which have led to it. The extreme conservatism of Rhode Island, first exhibited by the hesitancy with which she gave in her adhesion to the union of the States, is still more manifest in the fact that, until after 1840, she never had a Constitution of her own, but continued under the old colonial charter of 1663. The voters under the old regime included only possessors of real estate to the amount of $134, and their eldest sons. At first, because farming was the chief occupation of the people, and because younger sons who engaged in other employments, such as fishing, trading, smithing, etc., could easily purchase a homestead for a few hundred dollars, the restriction was scarcely felt to be a burden, and did not remove the control of affairs from the hands of the majority. But, in process of time, land in the villages augmented in value, and the number of persons engaged in occupations which did not require the ownership of real estate so increased that at the presidential election of 1840, in which the excitement probably exceeded the one just closed, it became painfully manifest that a minority of the people had for years been governing the State. The vote cast at that election, then the largest ever polled in the State, was 8,292, and yet the United States census of the same year gave the male adult population as about 25,000, thus showing that only one-third of all the men exercised the franchise. That a condition of affairs so different from what existed in other States, and so contrary to the principles upon which not only the general government, but also that of Roger Williams, had been based, should have given rise to

A WIDESPREAD FEELING OF DISCONTENT

cannot be wondered at. Consequently, all who were deprived of the suffrage, and, as the event proved, a majority of those who possessed it, were ready to engage in a movement for the extension of the franchise. The present Constitution was adopted in December, 1842. In the spring of 1843, the first vote cast for Governor in accordance with its provisions reached the high figure of 16,520, just double that of two and a half years before, and a clear majority of all the adult males. Thus, again, Rhode Island enjoyed popular government, stood in line with her sister States, in accord with the principles of '76, and her people were satisfied. Inasmuch as nearly all the citizens were native born, it seemed of little consequence that a clause should be inserted in the new Constitution requiring a real estate qualification of the foreign born. But, as time wore on, manufacturing establishments, employing chiefly persons of foreign birth, came to be the chief industry of the State. This change in the population, together with other restrictions, constitutional, legal and extra legal, in less than twenty years from the adoption of the Constitution, had again converted the government into one by a minority. Although the population has increased from 108,000 in 1840 to 276,000 in 1880, the average vote of the State but little exceeds the first one cast under the Constitution, in the year 1843. The present election is the fifth, of all that have ever been held, in which the total vote has risen above 20,000. Although the number of adult males now residing in the State is 77,000, the total vote last Tuesday, the largest ever cast here, and following the most heated campaign of this generation, was but little above 29,000; thus showing that nearly two thirds, or, more exactly, 48,000 men, did not reach the polls.

SUFFRAGE IN THE TOWNS AND CITIES.

To show more clearly the effect of the restricted suffrage, I will cite local instances. During fifteen years' residence in Rhode Island I have lived in three different towns, viz.: Pawtucket, Lincoln and Cumberland. By estimate from the State census of 1875 the number of adult males in the town of Pawtucket in November, 1876, was above 5,000; the total number of votes cast at the presidential election of that year—which then was the largest ever polled—was 2,100, leaving nearly 3,000 men who, chiefly because of restrictions upon the suffrage, did not vote. In the town of Lincoln the number of adult males exceeded 3,000; the vote was 767. In Cumberland the adult males numbered more than 1,500, the total vote 555. In the city of Providence, whose population is nearly two-fifths of that of the entire State, the number of adult males in 1876 was 30,000; the vote cast was 9,110. Since, at the above election a much greater number of votes were polled than in local elections, and since the opposition, as well as many members of the dominant party, objects to the existing limitation of the franchise, it may readily be seen how small the oligarchy which is controlling in the State, in the great city of Providence, and in the manufacturing towns and villages. Let us compare this with other States. In 1876, Florida, with 30,000 less inhabitants, cast 20,000 more votes than Rhode Island. In Iowa, a Republican stronghold, the ratio of the vote to the population was nearly as 1 to $4\frac{1}{2}$; in Louisiana, the ratio was as 1 to 5; in New York, as 1 to $4\frac{1}{2}$; in Mississippi, with all its bulldozing, as 1 to $5\frac{1}{2}$; in the whole United States, as 1 to $5\frac{1}{2}$; in Rhode Island, nearly as 1 to 10. The two members of Congress from this State have a smaller constituency of actual voters than one congressman in most of the other States. For example, the total vote of both of our districts in 1878 was 18,396, while in Massachusetts the average per district was 22,707, and in Connecticut, 26,089. Had our vote this year relatively equalled that thrown in Maine in September,—and with our compactness and unusually large proportion of adult males, it ought not to have been less—it would

4

have exceeded 61,000. Since the last presidential election the restrictions contained in the Constitution

HAVE BEEN INTENSIFIED BY LAW.

In addition to the two years necessary to gain a residence, an annual personal registration is now required of those who vote by payment of the tax of one dollar, and no one, except owners of real estate, can get their names upon the check-list *during the year in which the voting occurs*. Consequently, while in other States registration was taking place till within a few weeks or a few days of the great November contest, here it had to be done ten months previously, at a time when the party nominations had not been made, and when popular attention was not directed to the subject. As a result of this most effective restriction, multitudes of our native-born citizens, both Republican and Democratic, have been gnashing their teeth in vain regrets. To give a few illustrative cases coming within my own knowledge: a member of my own family, who last winter was attending a course of lectures in Philadelphia, and had neglected to register before leaving the State early in the autumn, is disfranchised for the entire year of 1880. A well-known physician of Providence, who was very desirous of depositing his vote for Garfield, could not do so, because in 1879 he did not think to register. The president of Brown University, after delivering two effective campaign speeches in behalf of the Republican ticket, found, to his surprise and chagrin, that his name was not upon the voting list, and, in response to his earnest inquiries whether he could not then register, was informed that the Constitution recognized no distinction of persons. In a similar predicament, I am informed, were fifty-five young men in our little village. At previous presidential contests the registry tax could be paid at any time prior to the last week before election as the State Constitution allows, but three years ago the Legislature fixed the second Saturday in January as the latest date of payment, and a failure to do so then debars from voting as effectually as if the riegstration itself had been neglected. But it is needless to dwell further upon the disqualification arising from a system of registration which, so far as I am aware, has no parallel elsewhere in the United States.

THE PROPERTY QUALIFICATION.

Citizens of foreign birth must own $134 worth of real estate in order to become voters. Now, few workingmen care to purchase real estate, except to make a homestead. In the vicinity of our village a low average for the cost of homesteads, which qualify the owners to vote, is $2,000, so that, practically, the latter large sum, instead of the nominal $134, is the investment required of our adopted citizens in order that they may be placed upon an equality with natives. What could Cicero have meant when, alluding to Roman citizenship, he said that a citizen by choice was equally worthy with a citizen by chance? How such a wholesale restriction acts in a State whose industries are plied by persons of foreign birth may easily be imagined. A neighbor of mine, born in Scotland, whose large family of workers render material aid in producing the cotton fabrics which enrich the State, says that he was completely confounded when, after moving here, he learned that he could not vote, and has seriously contemplated returning to Massachusetts, where he had hitherto lived and exercised the franchise. Another, also of Scotish birth, tells me that he voted for Taylor, and at seven successive presidential elections did not fail to cast his ballot in favor of the candidate of one or the other party. Nearly four years ago he moved into Rhode Island, and now at this, his eighth quadrennial election, he finds himself disqualified, because, forsooth, when a minor, he emigrated from another land of liberty to this one. Another, an Irishman, who moved here several years since, says he has voted for thirty years, but now cannot. However, a multiplication of individual examples is not necessary; look at the sum total. By the State census of 1875 the number of persons of foreign birth possessed of the qualification required by the Constitution in order to become voters was 5364. At that time, by estimate from the same source, there must have been 30,000 foreign born adult males in the State, or a disfranchisement of nearly five-sixths.

THE EXCUSE.

Is it asked, what excuse the small minority of citizens, who prefer a suffrage so greatly restricted, offer for thus departing from the fundamental principle of American institutions, that all governments " derive their just powers from the consent of the governed?" Their answer is, the danger which would accrue to good government from universal suffrage. It would seem to devolve upon them to show that we do possess an exceptionally superior government, that our elections are purer, and our public servants better, than those of other Commonwealths, where the franchise is free. This they cannot do On the contrary, during the twenty years that Rhode Island has been ruled by a minority, corruption in politics has been rife—as bad, perhaps worse, in proportion to the number of inhabitants, than in any other State. We have proved no exception to the rule that the pocket borough is the most easily bought and sold, a fact which furnishes a strong argument why, since our borders cannot be extended, we should increase the voting population by broadening the basis of suffrage. As to the quality of our public servants, suffice it to say that during the twenty years past of the men who have been sent to Congress one only, Hon. Thomas A. Jenckes, has acquired an enviable national reputation, while other States, with no better material for statesmen, have been represented during all that period by one or more men of international fame.

OUR DISFRANCHISED CITIZENS,

as a class, are in every way worthy to be made freemen. Whether native or foreign born, they inherit a love of liberty and a capacity for representative government. Little Rhody hums like a bee-hive with industry, and in no part of the world are there fewer drones; and yet the men who indirectly pay our taxes, who build our palatial residences, both public and private, who have made our State relatively the wealthiest in the Union, who have spilled their blood to save the nation in one war, and who, in in the event of another, will be the first to offer their lives for the common defence—these men are largely deprived of their political rights. That they keenly feel the degradation and injustice imposed upon them is unquestionable. After having been considered worthy, during the campaign, to parade by the thousand as Boys in Blue and Hancock Guards, and to stand for hours, night after night, listening to an exposition of the principles of the two parties, then when the time arrived for expressing at the ballot-box the convictions thus fostered, to have the door slammed in their faces was felt to be an insult. Nor is it a wise course to get up a full head of steam, and then shut the safety valve. Having heard from every stump, both Democratic and Republican, glowing tributes to equal rights, popular government and universal liberty, they found that two out of three—in all the State 50,000 men—did not succeed in approaching that "free ballot-box." As thinking men, many of whom have emigrated to this famed land of liberty, because its citizens were thought fit to govern themselves, they utter curses not loud, but deep. If they continue quietly to submit to the imposition, I will confess myself mistaken either in the men or in their sentiments. The disfranchised element has the earnest sympathy of the best minds in the State, of all who, though themselves possessing the franchise, yet regard the Declaration of Independence as something other than a glittering generality, of many who, taking part in the anti-slavery movement, are imbued and have inoculated their sons with those fundamental principles of our government, which were revived in the fervid utterances of its great leaders. Here, as elsewhere in New England, there is a profound belief in the axiom of Charles Sumner that, "Equality of rights is the first of rights," and in the sentiment of Abraham Lincoln that the rule of the minority is anarchy or despotism. In Rhode Island it is not anarchy.

THE ISSUE SIMPLE.

As I have said, scarcely a third of her men ever vote, and of that third only one-half (I make a liberal—in my opinion too liberal—allowance) at heart approve of the restricted suffrage which exists. If this be so, one-fifth of the people are ruling the other four-fifths—15,000 dominating 60,-000. The issue presented between those who favor the present status, and those who would change to "a government of the people, by the people and for the people" is so simple that the blindest need not mistake it. In conversation with an intelligent gentleman a short time since, I referred to the existing condition of affairs. "The suffrage is already too free," he said. "But," I replied, "our government is not what it professes to be, democratic." "Then let us change the name," was his rejoinder. I certainly agree with this outspoken man, that the name and the thing should correspond, that, if we are to have an oligarchy, no pretence should be made to anything else. But how many are ready to thus boldly take the position which logically is the true one ? How many voters of Rhode Island are prepared, at this late day, to renounce the Pilgrims' covenant taken by *foreigners* in the cabin of the Mayflower: "We agree, before God and each other, that the freely-expressed will of the majority shall be the law of all, which we will all obey?" Were there a strong minority among us sufficiently arrogant and egotistic to assert that our little community is right, and the rest of the 50,000,000 who compose this great nation wrong in form of government; or were there a majority here who, though aware that they are denied their political rights, are unprepared to make the needed effort to gain them, I should be ready to admit that we deserve the contempt which our neighbors have occasionally expressed for us.

ATTEMPTS TO AMEND THE CONSTITUTION.

But, it may be asked, in the twenty years of government by a minority, has no attempt been made to remedy the anomalous state of affairs? Yes, repeatedly, by amending the Constitution, and in vain. The last trial was in 1876, when a majority of the nearly 22,000 electors who voted on the matter did express a wish to abolish the property qualification, so far as it applied to soldiers and sailors of foreign birth who had served in Rhode Island regiments during the civil war. But our Constitution contains the provision that three-fifths of those who vote must approve a proposed amendment, in order that it may become a part of the organic law. When to this difficulty is added the necessity which exists that any desired change must be approved before submission to the people by a majority of all the members elected to each house in two successive Legislatures, it will readily be seen that our prospect of relief by this method is very faint. And, as a historical fact, any more radical measure of relief, such as the abolition of the registry tax or the substitution of an educational for the property qualification, has always failed to receive a majority of the votes, much less the three-fifths requisite.

Since amendments to the existing Constitution cannot be procured, the only available remedy lies in the formation of a new one. Very properly, the Constitution of Rhode Island provides no means by which a constitutional convention can be called. But no one, I presume, will say that, consequently, for all future time this State is debarred from framing another Constitution. The right is inherent and indefeasable. The only question open is as to the mode. Naturally, because the machinery is in its hands, the existing government is the instrument through which an invitation should be extended to the people to elect delegates to a convention. The first step, then, toward obtaining a government by the majority is a petition to the General Assembly to issue a call for a constitutional convention, seconded by an organized agitation which shall leave no room for the minority to misunderstand the wishes and determination of the people.

8

ADDENDUM.

A comparison of the census of 1880 and the presidential election of the same year shows in several of the States the following ratio of votes to population:

Maine, 1 to 4.5; New Hampshire, 1 to 4.0; Vermont, 1 to 5.1; Massachusetts, 1 to 6.3; Rhode Island, 1 to 9.4; Connecticut, 1 to 4.6; New York, 1 to 4.6; Ohio, 1 to 4.4; Iowa, 1 to 5.0; Delaware, 1 to 5.0; Florida, 1 to 5.1; Georgia, 1 to 9.8; Mississippi, 1 to 9.6; Louisiana, 1 to 8.7; United States (thirty-eight States), 1 to 5.3.

It is noticeable that the only States which at all approximate to Rhode Island in smallness of vote are the gulf States, where a large portion of the negroes did not go to the polls; also that in the whole United States more than two-thirds of the adult males actually voted, in Rhode Island but little more than one-third.

At the opening of the spring session (1881) of the General Assembly the first installment of a petition, which was eventually signed by over four thousand men of Rhode Island, was presented in the House of Representatives by John F. Tobey, Esq., a member from Providence. It read as follows:

To the Honorable the General Assembly:

The undersigned, men of Rhode Island, desiring that the suffrage in this State should be made equal and popular, and believing that the removal of the property qualification for voters now required of foreign-born citizens would be for the best interests of the State, do hereby petition your honorable body to call upon the people to elect delegates to a Constitutional Convention, to be held at an early date, in order that such reforms and other beneficial changes in the fundamental law may be accomplished.

On the 19th of January, when the first petition of over two thousand men was called up in the House of Representatives, two members of the Committee on the Judiciary expressed the opinion that the General Assembly had no right to call a constitutional convention, and favored its reference to their own committee, in order that this question of law might be determined.

Thus the subject became separated into two distinct questions: First, Has the General Assembly the right to provide for calling a constitutional convention? Secondly, Is it expedient to revise the Constitution? The first of these questions was argued before the committee by two well-known members of the bar, Mr. Allen and Mr. Gorman; and although they did not both speak at the first hearing, for the sake of unity, they are here brought together. The remarks of the other petitioners before the committee are given in the order of their presentation. For their preservation, we are indebted in part to the reports of the Providence press, and in part to the participants.

The Committee on the Judiciary were Messrs. Wm. P. Sheffield, Benjamin T. Eames, Benjamin N. Lapham, Le Baron B. Colt and John P. Gregory.

At the first hearing, which was held at noon on Monday, February 7th, but four of the petitioners appeared.

HENRY W. ALLEN, Esq., OF PROVIDENCE.

was the first speaker. He called attention to the fact that since the adoption of the present constitution of Rhode Island, thirty-one States have formed entirely new constitutions, and of the remaining six States, outside of Rhode Island, four of the six have held constitutional conventions. Only three of the States, Maine, Connecticut and Rhode Island, that were in existence in 1842, but have either adopted new constitutions or have held constitutional conventions for this purpose.

Thirty-seven out of the thirty-eight States allow the amendment of the constitution by a majority vote of the electors after the preliminary legislative steps have been completed. The one State standing alone in this regard is Rhode Island. All the other States have recognized their growth and progress, and the fact that the provisions of a constitution in 1842 are inadequate to the needs of the people in 1881. There are various changes necessary to be made in our constitution, notably a change in suffrage restrictions, a provision for the equalizing of taxation, a provision allowing Providence, which has nearly half the population, and pays nearly half the taxes in the State, more than twelve representatives; the abolishing of one of the present State capitals; the abolition of the May Session of the General Assembly; the granting the Governor a modified veto power; a provision prohibiting the enactment of retroactive laws; the abolition of the registry tax and the property qualification; allowing future amendments by a majority vote of the people; a provision permitting many things now done by the Assembly to be done under general laws, such as creating corporations, changing names, etc., and various other changes are needed.

The air is full of ideas for changes in the constitution, and every year there are petitions of one sort or another to the Assembly regarding the matter. A convention should be held for the sifting of these ideas, the adoption or rejection of each proposition, and the establishing of a new constitution for the State. The constitution, which was well in 1842, is entirely inadequate for the public of 1881.

There is no doubt as to the legality of the proposed constitutional convention, and as to the right of the Legislature to call it. The General

Assembly has the power and the right to call such a convention directly, or, if it see fit, to submit the calling of the convention to a vote of the people.

The sovereignty of the State resides in the people. The people cannot alienate that sovereignty. One generation cannot, by the adoption of any sort of a constitution, bind either itself or any future generation beyond recall. The people are sovereign, and have the right to change or alter their government as they see fit. This right is the corner-stone of our Republic. The constitution is the creature of the people. The power of the people to alter their constitution is set down in thirty-four State constitutions. Thus in the constitution of Vermont it is laid down:

"That government is, or ought to be, instituted for the common benefit, protection, and security of the people, nation, or community, and not for the particular emolument or advantage of any single man, family, or set of men, who are a part only of that community; and that the community hath an indubitable, unalienable, and indefeasible right to reform or alter government, in such manner as shall be by that community judged most conducive to the public weal."

In the constitution of Connecticut:

"That the great and essential principles of liberty and free government may be recognized and established, we declare:

"SECTION 2. That all political power is inherent in the people, and all free governments are founded on their authority, and instituted for their benefit; and that they have at all times an undeniable and indefeasible right to alter their form of government in such manner as they may think expedient."

In the constitution of Maryland:

"That all government of right originates from the people, is founded in compact only, and instituted solely for the good of the whole; and they have at all times the unalienable right to alter, reform, or abolish their form of government in such manner as they may deem expedient."

In the constitution of Ohio:

"All political power is inherent in the people. Government is instituted for their equal protection and benefit, and they have the right to alter, reform, or abolish the same whenever they may deem it necessary."

And so in almost identical language in the constitutions of thirty other States.

The agents of this sovereignty are, first, the electors; second, the Legislature; third, the constitutional convention; fourth, the executive, and fifth, the judiciary.

The constitutional convention is a part of the government of the several States. It is so recognized by jurists of the highest ability. Our political history shows it. Since the people are sovereign, and have a right to change their government and constitution as they see fit, there must be some means by which that change may be made. We find the means in the agents of the sovereignty. That is, in the Legislature, first, which has the right and the power to pass a law calling the constitutional convention into existence; second, the convention itself, which frames the new constitution; and, third, the electors, who pass upon the proposed constitution, and either adopt or reject it.

The convention cannot *make* a new constitution. It merely *proposes* one. It is the sovereign people alone who can make or unmake constitutions.

While the right and power of the Assembly to call a convention is clear from these general principles, laid down in so many constitutions, and recognized by all our jurists and statesmen, we also claim that that right and power is recognized by the constitution of our own State:

Section 1, Article 1, says: "In the words of the Father of his Country, we declare that 'the basis of our political systems is the right of the people to make and alter their constitutions of government; but that the constitution which at any time exists, till changed by an explicit and authentic act of the whole people is sacredly obligatory upon all.'" Section 23 of the same article says: "The enumeration of the aforegoing rights shall not be construed to impair or deny others retained by the people." Among them, said the speaker, is the right to change the fundamental law. Section 10 of Article 4 says: "The General Assembly shall continue to exercise the powers they have heretofore exercised, unless prohibited in this constitution." Previous to this convention the Legislature had called four conventions, in 1824, 1834, 1841 and 1842, so it appears the Legislature had this right before this. The charter did not give them this right, nor did Congress pass a law enabling them to do this. They called it in the power which they had as the sovereign people. The Legislature had exercised this power, and Section 10, Article 4, says the Legislature shall continue to exercise this power unless prohibited by this constitution. From the beginning to the end of the constitution there isn't a single section that says the Assembly shall not call a constitutional convention. As a right which they had under the charter, and not forbidden by the constitution, they have that right now.

We also find that this right has been heretofore recognized in this State, and is now for the first time called in question. In 1853 the General Assembly of Rhode Island twice submitted to the electors the question of whether or not a constitutional convention should be held. If they had that right in 1824, 1834, 1841, 1842, and twice in 1853, how comes it that they have not that same right in 1881? It is too late to question a right exercised by our Legislature six different times without denial.

If we examine the history of other States, we find the precedents all one way—in favor of the claim.

Twenty-five constitutional conventions in eighteen different States of this Union have been called under provisions precisely similar to the provisions of our constitution. Jameson in his able work on the Constitutional Convention says that a Legislature has an undoubted right, both from principle and uniform practice, to call a constitutional convention, either directly, or by first submitting the question to a vote of the people, although the existing constitution may contain a provision for specific amendments. Where a constitution simply provides for specific amendments, and sets forth how those amendments *may* be made, as the constitution of this State does, but does not explicitly forbid a convention or changes to be made in any other way, a convention to revise the entire constitution may be called by the Assembly. The ablest jurists of this country have maintained the right of a Legislature to call a convention under a constitution like ours.

In the case of *Wells v. Bain*, reported in *75 Penn. State Reports*, at page 39, Chief Justice Agnew gives an opinion wherein all the court concur, in which he says:

"Since the Declaration of Independence, in 1776, it has been an axiom of the American people, that all just government is founded in the consent of the people. This is recognized in the second section of the declaration of rights of the constitution of Pennsylvania, which affirms that the people 'have at all times an inalienable and indefeasible right to alter, reform or abolish their government in such manner as they may think proper.' * * * * * * * * * * * *

"The words, 'in such manner as they may think proper,' in the declaration of rights, embrace but three known recognized modes by which the whole people, the State, can give their consent to an alteration of an existing lawful frame of government, viz.:

1. The mode provided in the existing constitution.
2. A law, as the instrumental process of raising the body for revision and conveying to it the powers of the people.
3. A revolution.

The first two are peaceful means through which the consent of the people to alteration is obtained, and by which the existing government consents to be displaced without revolution. *The government gives its consent, either by pursuing the mode provided in the constitution, or by passing a law to call a convention.*"

The question whether upon principle, upon precedent or upon authority is almost too clear for argument. Certain it is, that the uniform practice of our sister States, the practice of past Legislatures of our own State, and the opinion of courts and jurists are in favor of the right claimed.

CHARLES E. GORMAN, Esq., of Providence.

Alderman Charles E. Gorman spoke as follows:

Mr. Chairman and Gentlemen of the Committee:

Had it not been for the declaration by one member of the House that the General Assembly had no power to grant the prayer of this petition, and of another member, that he should consider a vote in favor of a constitutional convention would be a violation of his oath of office, I suppose this honorable committee would not have been required to have performed the additional arduous duties which these hearings impose, but that it would have been referred to a special committee representing not so much the legal ability of the House as the different sections of the State, composed of members whose time is not so much engrossed with the duties of their committees.

I recognize, however, the wisdom of those who urged the reference of the petition to this committee for the purpose at least of settling the primary question of the constitutional powers of the General Assembly. In fact, when gentlemen so eminently learned in the law as the two to whom I have referred, question the constitutional powers of the present General Assembly, and impeach, at the same time, the acts of previous Legislatures, no other course could prevail than the one pursued.

As you are to sit, therefore, in some sense as the appelate court of the body of your appointment upon matters of this character, and on whose judgment, in a large degree, the legislative expression on this important question will depend, I deem it my duty to first address myself to the primary question raised.

The prayer is that a constitutional convention be convened for the pur pose of framing a new constitution for the State. The mode is left to the legislative judgment. The prayer in substance is, that whatever constitutional and legal mode exists for calling into being a convention to frame a new constitution be exercised by the General Assembly, recognizing that, regardless of whether there are other modes that can be exercised, at least the General Assembly has ample and sufficient power to so formulate in legal shape the right which our constitution declares to reside somewhere in the State, in the people at large, in the electors at large, or in the General Assembly as being the channel through which in peaceful mode this sovereign act can only be performed. Section 1, Article 1, declares "the basis of our political systems is the right of the people to make and alter their constitutions of government." It is not part of th present discussion to open the question of who compose the people above referred to. And I am confident whatever might be my own views upon that question, that it has been settled for the present, at least in Rhode Island, and he who would enter into that discussion with those who survive, with the recollection of the times and discussions that occupied the attention of Rhode Island at the time of the adoption of the present constitution needs to abandon all hope of changing the decision then made.

As this question is one of construction, let us examine it without bias, and see where its termination may lead. Should we agree with some, would we not only find that we had no power to obtain a new constitution, but also that we had none at all of binding force and legality, and that the danger of those whose consciences are disturbed is that if they follow out the positions they occupy, then they have sworn to support a constitution that is illegal and a piece of usurpation.

Historically considered, what has been the legal government of Rhode

Island in the past ? We commenced with the charters. The legislative power was reposed by those in a general assembly, but they delegated no absolute sovereign power, all legislation being subject to the restrictions of the charters. At the Revolution, the sovereign power of government passed to the people of Rhode Island, whoever they may be determined to be. And although the General Assembly claimed the most extraordinary powers of government, it always recognized that the freemen or land-owners of Rhode Island were the source of power and government, and not the whole people of Rhode Island. Now, if this was so, what greater right had the General Assembly in 1820, 1824, 1834, 1841 and 1842 to call constitutional conventions than the General Assembly of 1881?

In the charter there was no provision for amendment, or for change. How came, then, the General Assembly to call these conventions? It did so because it claimed that it was the only known channel through which this sovereign right of framing a constitution could be called into being, under a government of law. Now, if that argument was good in 1842, when the convention which framed our present constitution was carried, why unsound in 1881? If unsound in 1881, then the validity of our present constitution is in question. And it is no sufficient answer to say that that the ratification of this act of the General Assembly by the freemen cured the original usurpation, if there was one. For it cannot be decided now under what influences of duress and terror they may have voted or refrained from voting under the disturbed state of affairs of 1842. The few men who controlled the government of Rhode Island had peculiar views, and which were not fully in harmony with those established by the national constitution and held in the other States of the Union. One idea which always prevailed here was that the General Assembly of Rhode Island was a body similar to the British Parliament, having supreme power. It was a power which had been exercised for a long time, and the few people who had for two centuries maintained a government by a few, for a few, were opposed to a government of the people, by the people, and for the people, and in framing the present constitution it is well known that they strove to retain as much of the letter and spirit of the old form of government as they could in the face of the constitution of the United States and the agitation that was then shaking the State. And in accordance with that desire, and with that sole purpose, the 10th section of Article V. was incorporated, which is as follows:

"The General Assembly shall continue to exercise the powers they have heretofore exercised, unless prohibited in this constitution."

What powers are referred to? Those that had heretofore been exercised, not prohibited. Among those powers were the power to call a constitutional convention—it had been exercised on different occasions previous to 1842 and recognized as one of its powers and rights, and although some claimed the right of the people to assemble themselves, for the purpose of framing a constitution of government, that right was not claimed as the only mode in which a convention could be assembled.

Another power that had long been exercised was a judicial power of granting new trials. This power had been exercised since 1680, notwithstanding the objection and complaints of the British Home Government, down until the adoption of the constitution, and was continued until 1856. The power, however, came to be questioned, and twice have the judges of the Supreme Court given their opinion on the question—in the opinion of the judges on the constitutionality of "An act to reverse and annul the judgment of the Supreme Court of Rhode Island for treason rendered against Thomas W. Dorr, June 25, A. D. 1844," passed at the January session of the General Assembly, A. D. 1854,—Section 3, R. I. Report, page 300. And again in the case of Taylor & Co. *vs.* Place, 4 R. I., page 324. In this last case the Supreme Court decided that, although the General Assembly had exercised judicial powers prior to the adoption of the constitution, it was prohibited from exercising any such powers now by force of Article 10. In regard, however, to the power of the General Assembly the precedents are numerous. In 1820, 1824, 1834, 1841 and 1842, bills were passed by the General Assembly providing for constitutional conventions. This power had always been claimed to be the exclusive right of the General Assembly and is nowhere prohibited. And since the constitution it has been exercised on two occasions, in May, 1853, and September, 1853. This shows what interpretation those who were members, in a great measure, of the convention which framed the constitution put upon their work, and what they understood was one of the powers continued in the General Assembly.

Without, however, this clear language of Section 10, Article 5, and of this uniform exercise of the power, can there be any serious question of the legislative power in the premises? The right to amend and revise a constitution are distinct powers. While upon the submission of a single isolated amendment many might refuse to vote for it without the other necessary changes which would harmonize with the proposed change, upon the question of a revision of the constitution by a convention of delegates elected for the specific purpose of framing a complete constitution, all matters would be arranged to make an harmonious instrument.

And as the power to amend must emanate from the General Assembly in the mode prescribed, the power to call into being a constitutional convention belongs to the general powers of the legislative branch of a government, through which the voice of sovereignty can only lawfully speak. And so in the past in twenty-eight instances have the General Assemblies of different States, without any provision in their constitutions for the calling of conventions, exercised this right as one of their legitimate powers, viz.: In Georgia, in 1789, 1838 and 1879; South Carolina, 1790; New Hampshire, 1791; New York, 1801, 1821, 1846; Connecticut, 1818; Massachusetts, 1820, 1853; Rhode Island, 1820, 1824, 1834, 1841, 1842, May 1853, September 1853; Virginia, 1829, 1850, 1864; North Carolina, 1835; Pennsylvania, 1837; New Jersey, 1844; Missouri, 1845, 1861, 1865; Indiana, 1850.

In Indiana's constitution, however, there was a provision that a convention should be called every twelfth year, and although the twelve years had not expired the Legisture called the convention which passed the constitution of that State of 1851.

The view which has always been held by the General Assembly of Rhode Island is very well evidenced by the action of the General Assembly when the Superior Court of Rhode Island declared the "force act," so called, to be unconstitutional in Trevett vs. Weeden in 1786. By the above act the General Assembly abolished the trial by jury in cases arising under that act, and the court declared they had no power to deprive the accused of the right of trial by jury, which was secured by the charter. Upon the announcement of the decision of the court, a great outcry followed this attempt of the court to sit in judgment upon an act of the General Assembly. The Assembly was convened at once, and it was resolved that the court had "declared and adjudged an act of the supreme Legislature of this State to be unconstitutional and so absolutely void; and, whereas it is suggested that the aforesaid judgment is unprecedented in this State, and may tend to abolish the legislative authority thereof," the judges were ordered to appear before the Assembly and defend their judgment. They appeared and gave their reasons, upon hearing which the Assembly resolved that no sufficient reasons had been given, and when the terms of the judges expired at the end of the year, they supplanted four of the five judges by others who would in the future not question the supreme power of the General Assembly to do all things.—Arnold's History of Rhode Island, Vol. 2, chap. 24.

Thus it appears that the most extreme legislative power was very early claimed and asserted by the General Assembly of Rhode Island. That the General Assembly always possessed and now possesses, unless prohibited, complete legislative powers will not be contended. One of those those powers is the one now asked to be exercised. Mr. Cooley, in his work on "Constitutional Limitations," p. 31, speaking of this power, says:

"In the original States, and all others subsequently admitted to the Union, the power to amend or revise their constitutions resides in the great body of the people as an organized body politic, who, being vested with ultimate sovereignty, and the source of all State authority, have power to control and alter the law which they have made at their will. But the people, in the legal sense, must be understood to be those who, by the existing constitutions, are clothed with political rights, and who while that instrument remains, will be the sole organs through which the will of the body politic can be expressed.

"But the will of the people to this end can only be expressed in the legitimate modes prescribed by the constitution by which revision or amendment is sought, *or by an act of the legislative* department of the State, which alone would be authorized to speak for the people upon this subject, and to point out a mode for the expression of their will in the absence of any provision for amendment or revision contained in the constitution itself."—See 6 Cushing, 573; Collier *vs.* Frierson, 24, Ala, 100.

" We entertain no doubt," says the court in the above case, " that to change the constitution *except* by a convention, every requisition which is demanded by the instrument itself must be observed."—See also Jameson on Constitutional Conventions, §§ 415, 420, 479 and 520; also 21, N. Y., 9.

Judge Cooley in his above mentioned work, page 87, speaking of the powers of the Legislature, says: " In creating a legislative department and conferring upon it legislative power, the people must be understood to have confined the full and complete powers as it rests in, and may be exercised by, the sovereign power of any country, subject only to such restrictions as they may have seen fit to impose, and to the limitations which are contained in the constitution of the United States. The legislative department is not made a special agency for the exercise of especially defined legislative powers, but is entrusted with the general authority to make laws at discretion."

In People *vs.* Draper, 15 N. Y., 543, Denis Ch. J. says: "The people in framing the constitution committed to the Legislature the whole law making power of the State, which they did not expressly or impliedly withhold. Plenary power in the Legislature, for all purposes of civil government, is the rule."

Redfield, C. J , in 27 V. 142, says: " It has never been questioned, so far as I know, that the American Legislatures have the same unlimited power in regard to legislation, which resides in the British Parliament, except where they are restrained by written constitutions. The people must, of course, possess all legislative power originally. They have committed this in the most general unlimited manner to the several State Legislatures, saving only such restrictions as are imposed by the constitution of the United States or of the particular State in question."

With these quotations and references, together with what I may have feebly shown of our past history and action upon this question, I feel I have assisted the committee in coming to these conclusions:

1. That the Legislature of Rhode Island previous to the adoption of the present constitution exercised the power we now evoke;

2. That by careful and intended provision the people have continued that power to it;

3. That the Legislature has recognized that continuance by having exercised it;

4. That apart from any delegation of that power or any prohibition of its exercise, the power exists as one of the necessary and general powers of the legislative department of American governments, and that therefore it clearly appears that the General Assembly has ample and full constitutional power to grant the prayer of the petitioners.

In this discussion I have not referred, nor need I at the present stage, to what the details of the legislation in calling a convention shall be. They rest in a great measure in the legislative judgment, always remembering

3

that sovereignty ultimately rests in the people and all legislation should secure to them or a majority of them to express their sovereign will.

I do not propose to occupy any of the time of the committee in discussing the demands and needs for a convention. There are others present who will do that. The different suggestions of changes are numerous, and have been continuously advocated by greater or less numbers for the past fifteen years, and I do not, by mentioning them, make myself the special advocate of all. Besides manhood suffrage, there is woman's suffrage; the substitution of a poll tax for the present registry tax; the removal of the liquor question from local and State politics by fixing an established rule for at least ten years, at the end of which the question of change may be submitted to the people; the abolition of Newport as a capital which exists as an expensive occasion for pastime alone; the creation of biennial sessions of the General Assembly, and other reforms and changes.

And whatever the committee may determine as to the feasibility of a convention, I trust at least that they will not determine that by the present constitution the people of Rhode Island have so parted with their sovereign rights that they are deprived of the right which is enjoyed by the people of every other State "to alter and amend their constitution," but rather that the constitutional rights and privileges that were enjoyed under the charter government are preserved in full to the people of Rhode Island to-day.

Dr. L. F. C. GARVIN, of Lonsdale,

spoke after Mr. Allen. He said that this hearing would have opened with an explanation of the terms of the petition were it not that the question had been raised in the House whether the General Assembly had the power to call a constitutional convention. This unexpected objection had made proper and indeed necessitated the legal statement of the gentleman who has preceded me. In addition to Mr. Allen's exhaustive statement, he felt at liberty to quote from a private letter addressed to himself, the following opinion of a distinguished lawyer in this city:

"I have no doubt that an act of the General Assembly, inviting the qualified electors of the State, assembled by delegates in a convention to frame a constitution to be submitted to the people of the State for their approval would be a lawful proceeding. Nor have I any doubt that such a convention ought to hold. Therefore I have signed a petition that the General Assembly would pass such an act."

Signed,   ABRAHAM PAYNE.

Dr. Garvin thought it proper that the grounds upon which the petition was based should be stated to the committee. One request of the petitioners was that the suffrage in this State should be made *popular*. A government by the people was the American theory. That idea presided at the birth of the United States, as well as at that of both the great parties now existing, the Democratic and the Republican.

Commencing on board the Mayflower, Winthrop, Alden and the other pilgrims covenanted as follows: " We agree before God and each other that the freely expressed will of the majority shall be the law of all, which we will all obey."

Roger Williams, in a letter written from Providence to the General Assembly in 1666, said: " The second jewel is liberty," including " liberty of society or corporation, of sending or being sent to the General Assembly, of choosing and being chosen to all offices and of making or repealing all laws and constitutions among us." Washington in his farewell address; Jefferson in the Declaration of Independence reiterated the same sentiments. The war cry of the Revolution was " No taxation without representation." The fame of Abraham Lincoln and Charles Sumner is due to their devotion to the single idea of popular liberty.

President elect Garfield has said: " You talk about the sovereign States or even the sovereign nation. A corporation is not a sovereign. The corporation that we call Ohio was made by the people, and they are its sovereigns; even the grand corporation that we call the United States was created also by the people who are its superiors, and its only sovereigns."

Such, said Dr. Garvin, is our theory; what now is our practice? The question comes, is the suffrage in our State " popular?" Of all the States in the Union, except a few in the extreme South, this is the only one in which at the last Presidential election a majority of the adult males did not vote. It is true that a majority of the electors did vote, but 48,000 men did not reach the polls. Had this State cast as many votes in proportion to its population as did Maine or New Hampshire, or New York, or New Jersey, or Ohio, or Indiana and other States, it would have polled upwards of 60,000; it did cast less than 30,000. In the city of Providence reside more than 30,000 adult males, but her vote has never reached 10,000. Only 15,000 possess the constitutional qualifications of electors, and more than 5,000 of those were absent from the polls in the exciting Presidential election just passed, mainly in consequence of impediments placed by the constitution and laws in the way of registration and the payment of the registry tax. Thus the suffrage is not " popular." The government is a government of a minority.

The petitioners also asked that our government should be made *equal*. That this, too, is our theory was shown by the fact that sentiments of equality were heard from every stump during the recent Presidential campaign, both Republican and Democratic. For example he quoted from a report of speeches made by three gentlemen at a meeting for workingmen, held at the headquarters of the Central Republican Club on the evening of October 2, 1880. Mr. Elisha Dyer, Jr., then said: " When we contrast the condition of the workingmen of this country with those of other nations, the honorable position they here enjoy, and the vast influence they possess, it seems but right that their aid should be invoked in the interests of that party which knows no rich, no poor, discriminates against no race, no color."

Mr. George M. Carpenter, Jr., the second speaker, said: "Whenever a party interferes with the political rights of a people, it ought to be utterly destroyed. [Applause.] The Republican party has ever had one ruling set of principles—equal rights for all. And in the language of General Garfield, 'next to liberty, the most sacred thing is labor.' The speaker concluded by saying 'If I could sum up in a word the principles of the Republican party, I would say, Preserve your liberty and your labor is safe.' [Applause.]"

The third and concluding speaker, John F. Tobey, Esq., closed by saying, "We must do what is right, and labor and strive that every man throughout the length and breadth of this land shall have the rights of a freeman." [Applause.]

At the same place, a week later, Rev. Wm. H. Channing, of London, spoke: "I want to show," said the speaker, "how the Republican party is the real democracy of this nation. This party knows three grand words, 'liberty, fraternity and equality.' Now the real democracy of this nation is the party who are true to those three great principles."

To these noble sentiments the petitioners say, amen.

Dr. Garvin asked what was meant by the term so often used, "equal rights." It could only mean that no discrimination should be made between one man and another because of any accidental and unimportant difference in them. For instance, the constitution of the United States forbids distinction between men on account of color, an accidental quality which has no influence upon good citizenship. So the place of a man's birth is not material, and the principle of equal rights allows no discrimination to be made in consequence of it. The five years' residence which the United States naturalization law requires of persons born abroad may be held as a full equivalent of the period of minority demanded of natives. Both are a time of probation in which an acquaintance with the institutions of the country is to be formed. But the real estate qualification imposed by the constitution of Rhode Island upon voters of foreign birth is the equivalent of nothing; it is grossly inequitable, just as unjust as it would have been at the close of the war to have required at the South a property or educational qualification of the blacks, and not of the whites.

He could understand how a Republican might favor a limited suffrage, such as would result from an educational qualification applied to all who might in future become voters; but he could not conceive how an intelligent disciple of Lincoln, Sumner, Chace, Greeley and Garrison could uphold the real estate requirement of the Rhode Island constitution.

The petition furthermore expresses the opinion that the removal of the real estate qualification "would be for the best interests of the State." Could any one claim that the State would in the end benefit itself by doing an injustice? Many of the most intelligent citizens of foreign birth, pre- -

ferring to go where they can have their rights, the State loses their services.

He spoke in this line for some moments, and then considered briefly other changes that seem to be needed in the constitution. The provision requiring a two years' residence after a removal into this State was thought to be a hardship. To him the question was a matter of principle, but many were interested in the practical effects which would result from the extension of the suffrage. This he believed to be a problem of the future which no one could certainly determine, but he himself had no doubt that so long as the wealth and intelligence of the State was included in one party that party would prevail.

The following tables he believed to be approximately correct:

TABLE A.
Voters according to nativity.

	Present suffrage.	Universal suffrage.
Total	46,000*	69,000
Of American birth	40,000	42,000
Of foreign birth	6,000	27,000
Of Irish birth	3,800	14,000
Of other nationalities	2,200	13,000

In table B the number of foreigners is estimated from the census of 1875, hence it would have been possible for them all to be naturalized at the present time. But as a matter of fact a large proportion of them have not as yet declared their intentions to become citizens, and consequently must reside here at least two years longer before voting.

TABLE B.
Voters reckoned by parentage.

	Universal suffrage.	Illiterate.	Educational qualification.
American	36,000	720	35,000
Foreign	30,000	4,200	25,000
Irish	19,000	2,850?	16,900
British American	3,500	1,260	2,000
Other nationalities	7,500	(500?)	7,000

It is a fact that foreigners and their children are now a majority in this State. So far as he knew no son of a foreign-born citizen had refused to sign this petition. Might not this majority, in accordance with the American principle of popular rule, more rightfully place a property qualification upon us? This they did not ask, they only plead for equality.

---

* The 46,000 voters include all who by registration could qualify. The whole number actually qualified for the year 1881 is 31,065. Thus, owing to the peculiarly obstructive system of registration explained in the early pages of this pamphlet, about 15,000 native men are now disfranchised.

Mr. Eames enquired of Dr. Garvin what other changes he would have made in the constitution besides in the property qualification, and in the two years' residence. He replied, disclaiming to speak for any other petitioner than himself, that a majority vote should be able to amend the constitution rather than the present three-fifths; that registration should be permitted nearer the time of election than now; that a poll tax should be substituted for the present registry tax; that the representation of the city of Providence should be in proportion to its population.

Mr. J. B. MARSH, of Central Falls.

I appear before you, gentlemen, to-day as a representative of the disfranchised class in this State on account of birth. The question has been often asked during the circulation of this petition, why ask for a convention when an amendment to the constitution would meet your requirements? We answer, that such amendments have been before the people on several occasions and been defeated, not, we believe, because the voters of this State are satisfied with the present restrictions of the franchise pertaining to foreign-born citizens, but on account of the conservatism which objects to removing the property qualification without offering anything in its stead. So, we think, if a constitutional convention could be held, such changes would be made in the constitution as would meet the conservatism, on the one hand, and satisfy those who wish to see the removal of the restrictions on the suffrage, on the other. We do not desire that restrictions should be entirely removed, we do not believe it would be for the best interest of the State so to do; but, we desire to see the property qualification removed, and in its stead an educational qualification. Again, the question is often asked, Is it an injustice that is placed upon the foreigner in this State; is it asking too much that he should own $134 worth of real estate to become a voter? I answer most emphatically that we regard it as an injustice and a great hardship. We regard it as an injustice first, because we believe it is contrary to the principle of a republican form of government; secondly, because we believe that no greater restriction should be placed upon the citizen of foreign birth in this State than in the other States of the Union. We regard it as a great hardship, because, while the sum nominally is $134, the real amount is much larger. I am informed by those who claim to know that when the property qualification was incorporated into the constitution for $134 you could purchase half an acre of land in Providence, and an acre in such places as Pawtucket and Central Falls, which was alike profitable for a homestead or cultivation.

It is said there are 10,000 to 15,000 foreign-born citizens in the city of Providence who cannot vote on account of the property qualification. Where, gentlemen, we ask in all earnestness, can any of these men qualify themselves to become voters in the city limits for $134? And, as it is not profitable for the operative or the mechanic to invest in real estate, except for a homestead, we would respectfully ask you, gentlemen, where in any of the manufacturing centres in this State can a homestead be bought for $134? Surely not in Newport, or Pawtucket, or Central Falls, or Woonsocket, or Bristol, or Warren, or River Point, or any of the leading manufacturing places, where live the most of those who are thus disfranchised. I have found on inquiry that within a quarter of a mile of the residence I now occupy in Central Falls a lot cannot be purchased with 50 feet front and 150 feet back for less than $1,000. I need hardly say to gentlemen of your experience that it would be an unwise thing to put a house on so expensive a lot of less value than $2,000. So, gentlemen, it becomes to the foreign-born citizen not a matter of $134, but a matter of from $2,000 to $3,000. The question is asked, is that too much to require? Cannot that even be acquired? Well, gentlemen, we will not undertake to say that it cannot be; but at what a price? At the *sacrifice* of the *education* of our children. It is a fact that cannot be denied, that those who acquire the qualification first are those who have the largest families of children, who, with little or no regard for their education, are sent to the mill and to the work-shop when they should be at school, or almost in their mothers' arms. There is another way that it can and often is accomplished, by engaging in a questionable traffic, sometimes under the shadow of the law, sometimes in defiance of it. But the Rhode Island constitution ignores all that. Its principle seems to be, get a homestead lawfully and honestly if you can, *but get it if you would vote*. So I assert, if a man who has to labor for his daily wages wishes to give his children an education, that they may become good citizens, to make his home comfortable and his family respectable, it is impossible to meet the requirements of the constitution to become a voter.

I know an operative, engaged in the same line of labor as myself in one of the mills at Lonsdale, who has one son now occupying an honorable rectorship in this State and another son now at college, who has said to me that he finds it impossible to educate his children and obtain the property qualification. [During the reference to the above operative his son, the Rev. Henry Hague, entered, and at the close of the speaker's remarks came down upon the floor and spoke strongly against the property restrictions in the constitution.]

I am acquainted with another operative, who has raised a large family, some now holding good positions in this city, one occupying an honorable Baptist pulpit in a neighboring State, who has never been able to vote, and who says he never expects to, unless the restrictions are removed from the constitution. I could enumerate by the score, if necessary, but one example is as good as a thousand. I can assure you, gentlemen, that there is a deep feeling in the hearts of all self-respecting foreigners in this State with regard to this embargo placed by the constitution on their birth. If this was a test of our loyalty to American institutions, or of our intelligence, we would not object, but when the stigma is placed upon our poverty, we ask you to remove it. I can remember how we used to hear, on the other side of the Atlantic, of that grand principle that all men are free and equal; but the foreign citizens of Rhode Island to-day asks whether it was not a fallacy. Especially is this thought impressed upon their minds when they remember that the suffrage laws are freer in England to-day than here. Let any man there become a resident householder for six months and pay his taxes he becomes entitled to the same political privileges as a native-born citizen. And yet this statement is not true of any other State in the Union but this.

Let me give another illustration of the unjust working of this property qualification: Sixteen years ago, when I came to this country and settled in Rhode Island, having lived in it ever since, a youth who worked with me stepped into my place when I came away. Ten years later that same young man came to this country, but landing on the politically more hospitable shores of Massachusetts, to-day he is a representative to the General Assembly of that State, with no more property, with no better education than myself, and yet I have never been allowed to *cast a ballot in Rhode Island*. We ask you, gentlemen, to candidly consider our petition, to consider it without the predjudice that has so long existed in this State against us. We are not that disloyal, dangerous element it has pleased a portion of the Providence press so often to slander us with being, in its appeals to the predjudices of the people against us. The late rebellion found its relatively most numerous opponents from this State in this element. In the late campaign for President, among the Boys in Blue, how many of this class were to be found? Why, sir, in Pawtucket, among the Union veterans, one was most conspicuous because he had to carry his torch in his left hand, his good right arm having been given to his country's service, yet he was amongst the first signers of this petition, as a non voter. Again, I am acquainted with a father and two sons who went to the war; the father was killed, the sons came home at the close of the rebellion to support the mother and younger members of the family, and to-day in this State those two sons cannot vote because they have no property.

Much more might be said, but we do not wish to trespass too long upon your time. But we ask you again to listen to our cry for justice. We believe it to be only a matter of time when this inequity will be swept from the constitution. The sons of foreigners are every year swelling the voting list more and more, and the time is not far distant when they will come in the strength of their manhood and their American citizenship and vote against that party which has done nothing to remove this wrong. I am no communist, no revolutionist, but I am a believer in that grand old principle so often enunciated, that all men are free and equal. I am a believer in that equally Republican principle, that the governed should have a voice in the choice of their governers, and that the citizen by choice has equal rights with the citizen by chance.

25

Rev. HENRY HAGUE, of Manville,

was called upon as the son of the man referred to by Mr. Marsh. He said he was in favor of free suffrage. He cannot vote in Rhode Island, but when he was in college in Massachusetts he paid his tax and voted. He had, he said, the fortune or the misfortune to be born in England. He came over here and served three years in the navy, from the time he was eighteen until he was twenty-one, and then went to college, where, as already stated, he had the right to vote. He came to Rhode Island, having been a candidate for holy orders for this diocese, and had been assigned to the diocese, and was trying to do his work. He had never entered politics at all. He had been told that if he bought $134 worth of real estate he might vote, but he should never buy a cent's worth of real estate in order to become a voter in this State. If his intelligence, his honesty, his life are not sufficient guarantee of his ability to vote he never should buy $134 worth of real estate, and so he never expected to become a voter in Rhode Island. He thought that if this right should be granted he should in gratitude cast his first vote for the party which gave the right. The time will come, he thought, when outside pressure or inside pressure will compel the Legislature to give this right.

Just before the second hearing of the petitioners before the Judiciary Committee of the House, Hon. H. B. Anthony delivered in the Senate of the United States a speech which he termed a "Defence of Rhode Island," the first paragraph of which was as follows:

"Mr. President—There are persons within and without, mainly without the State, who are calling upon Congress to interpose its authority in guaranteeing a Republican form of government in Rhode Island, on account of our constitutional limitations upon the suffrage Those who clamor on this matter from without the State are clearly meddling with what is not their proper concern; those within have mainly come from other States and countries, attracted by the advantages of a residence in Rhode Island, and belong to a class which has been happily described as composed of men who came among us uninvited, and 'on whose departure there is no restraint.' "

When it is remembered that more than half of the present adult population of Rhode Island was born without her borders, it cannot be wondered at that the discourtesy (to use a mild term) contained in the above quotation has created a wide-spread indignation. It is not too much to say that the class against whom the closing words are directed universally regards them as a gratuitous insult, a feeling which manifested itself repeatedly in the subsequent hearings.

The second hearing occurred on Monday, February 14, and for the convenience of workingmen, who are especially interested, was held in the evening. The legal argument of Mr. Gorman, who opened this hearing, has already been given. Eight other gentlemen spoke, as follows:

Mr. JOHN D'ARCY, OF APPONAUG.

Mr. Chairman and Gentlemen of the Committee:

I learn that your committee has a great deal of other business in hand besides this question of suffrage, and for that reason I will be very brief in my remarks. It has been said by the professional politicians, and repeated by some people who have neither time nor capacity for thinking, that if the real estate restriction on the suffrage is removed the gates are opened for a flood of ignorance at the polls. Now my idea of intelligence in an industrial community is its earning power. Of the many manufacturing industries in the State employing many thousands of foreign-born men I happen to be particularly acquainted with one industry, and that is calico printing. Within thirty-five minutes ride of where you sit, Mr. Chairman, there are seven large establishments engaged in that business, whose aggregated annual sales approach twenty millions of dollars; employing hundreds of men at salaries ranging from fifteen hundred to ten thousand dollars a year in the various chemical and mechanical processes necessary to the success of the business. The very nature of the business is such as to require a high degree of chemical and mechanical skill and knowledge. The fierce rivalry of competing establishments in other States, together with the continually fresh discoveries in the art and science of printing and dyeing, compel the men who have their money invested in that business to be perpetually recruiting the ranks of their skilled help, not only from other States, but from Europe also. Now I think I am stating the fact when I say that of all the men whose brains are necessarily engaged in producing results which bring into the State, from this one industry, the enormous sum of close to twenty millions of dollars a year, not one of them was born on American soil. Not one of these men can exercise all the political rights of a citizen in Rhode Island unless he owns real estate. Numbers of these men are American citizens under the naturalization laws, and have been voters in other States. Numbers of them have not qualified as citizens of the United States, knowing that the suffrage law of Rhode Island, in a measure, nullifies the naturalization laws of the nation. Now when it is remembered that the men to whom I refer are, of necessity, chemically and mechanically well educated, and of like necessity possessing a high type of intelligence, I ask you, in all conscience, do you believe that by allowing these men to vote the gates are opened for a flood of ignorance at the polls? Are these the men described as being dangerous to good government in Rhode Island, by the professional, ornamental and non-producing politicians? Over a dozen years residence in this State has made me very well acquainted with most of these men, and I have yet to find one who is satisfied with, or approves of the suffrage law of Rhode Island. Every man with whom I have conversed on the subject feels that the restriction is a most unjust and undeserved reproach cast upon him. It is believed and it is felt that when a man is compelled to place a given amount of property for public inspection as a prerequisite for exercising the franchise, the men who compel him to make such an exhibition force him into an ignominious position politically, and, to an extent, socially. The feeling is embittered when it is remembered that to foreign-born citizens alone, and in Rhode Island exclusively, is this property restriction applied. Is it to be wondered at, therefore, that men of intelligence and skill, whose services are constantly in demand in the arts, prefer to live where the laws are equal and popular as affecting the suffrage. It must not occasion surprise if it is found that in many branches of Rhode Island industry, capitalists have to pay higher wages for a certain type of operative skill than is paid by capitalists in like business in other States. Nor must it occasion surprise if it is found that men of brains, brought at great expense with their families from beyond the Atlantic or from distant parts of our own country to Rhode Island, because capital is in need of, and must have their skill; men who locate here intending to spend their days doing what in them lies to build up the manufacturing industries and increase the wealth of the State, it must not be a matter of surprise, I say, if such men feel aggrieved with the suffrage law of this State. Men of this stamp see their friends and acquaintances in other States, after five years' residence in the Republic, enjoying all the privileges and exercising all the rights of freemen, whilst here such men may spend a life time wearing a badge of political inferiority, kept on them by the politicians for their own selfish ends.

Mr. Chairman, we who are compelled to stay away from the polls cannot understand how the people of all the other States in the Union where the suffrage laws are equal and popular can be unwise, while the people of Rhode Island alone are wise with a suffrage law, which is confessed to be neither equal nor popular. We do not see that life or property is safer or any better guarded here than is life and property in any other New England State. We have a firm belief that if the people of Rhode Island get a fair opportunity, without the customary chicanery of the politicians, to vote on this question of suffrage, the time is close at hand when foreign-born citizens will vote without a property qualification. Now I feel entirely justified in stating from a long experience with business men in Providence and other places, that the politicians and not the people are the cause of keeping from the polls large numbers of men whose brains are daily employed in adding to the wealth and to the comfort of the inhabitants of the State. If, however, these same politicians will at length exercise even common foresight and assist in doing simple justice, the party they profess or affect to serve, has nothing to fear from an equal and popular suffrage. Nine-tenths of the men to whom I have referred as being cut off from the polls are Republicans, and in full sympathy with that great national party. These men would undoubtedly vote the Republican ticket as against all other tickets.

Speaking for myself, I say that I am liberal in religion and Republican in politics. I have lived many years in Massachusetts and some few in New Hampshire. In both these States I always upheld the Republican party. I would now, in any State in the Union other than Rhode Island, vote the Republican ticket, first, last and always. I believe in that party because it is the party of intelligence and progress. I regard self-defence as man's first duty. When, therefore, the Republican party in Rhode Island, or, more properly speaking, a fragment of that party, having the power to restore to me the privilege I am deprived of, one which could be exercised in any other State, neglects or refuses to do me justice, I say that under all circumstances I am opposed to that party here, until justice is done me politically. When that justice is done, I shall consider it an honorable duty to uphold and defend the Republican party of the State and nation. Mr. Chairman, we who are not professional politicians, we of the disfranchised class, ask that this stigma of a real estate qualification be removed. We who are loyal to the State and to the nation, industrious, law-abiding, self-supporting and intelligent, ask that we be no longer subjected to what we believe is a degrading mark before our fellow-men. We entreat you to do all possible in providing a way whereby the people of Rhode Island can act understandingly upon this question of equal and popular suffrage. We have absolute faith in the sense of honor and love of fair play inherent in the breasts of Rhode Island men. Let the people speak in convention. Who is it that fears to let the sovereign people pass judgment? Who, in the light of current events in other States, possessing even ordinary sagacity and foresight, will come forward and say the people *must* do one thing or leave undone another? We ask a verdict at the hands of the people in convention. When that verdict is given we will respectfully bow to the will of the people. No, I do not advocate the removal of all restriction on the suffrage by any means. Ignorance, by which I mean want of intelligence, should have no part in the franchise. I would have an educational qualification applied to all, wherever born. My idea of an educational test is not the mere mechanical writing of one's name or spelling some common word parrot-like. I would have the proposed voter write from dictation a paragraph of perhaps twenty lines from a newspaper, and I would have this done in the presence and by authority of an inspector appointed by the State. This, to my mind, would be a fair and a sufficient test. I take it, of course, that the applicant is a naturalized citizen if of foreign birth, and has resided the proper time within the State. I would not deprive any native-born citizen, who has heretofore voted, of that privilege because he could not stand the educational test, but all new voters, wherever born, should stand the educational test. These are in a crude way my views of a proper restriction. A lawyer would, no doubt, present them differently, from a like standpoint.

Now, one other point, and I will take up your time no longer. It is well known that the cause of education is in anything but a flourishing condition in the towns and villages of the State. Want of funds is the crying evil. One of the proverbs bequeathed to us by the fathers of the republic is that taxation without representation is tyranny. This must be said of Rhode Island, that if she does not allow a part of her people to vote she places no direct tax on them. Taxation and protection is somewhat different from taxation and representation. Now, I think I am right in stating that a poll tax is assessed and collected in all other States from male adults, whether citizens or foreigners, but the right to vote is religiously guaranteed to foreigners when they shall have become naturalized. Upon this explicit guarantee the States tax these people. And very properly as I think. Now, I speak from the records when I say that in the village where I reside the school has lost in the past dozen years over forty-six hundred dollars, owing to the fact that this State does not impose a poll tax. If there had been a poll tax collected yearly and put at interest, the sum on January 1, 1881, would have amounted to nearly seven thousand dollars. Every dollar of this forty-six hundred would have come from that class disfranchised by the suffrage law. Thousands of foreign-born men come into our manufacturing and commercial centres, as well as into the agricultural districts, stay for years and years and never pay one cent of direct tax. Not one cent do these men pay towards schools, roads, or any other object of public benefit and utility. Now, would it not benefit the cause of education immensely to assess and collect a poll tax annually on the just basis of an equal and popular suffrage as in other States? Under the present system the mortgaged homestead and the struggling farmer has to bear nearly all, if not quite all, the burden of schools and roads in the rural districts. And this system the farmers are told by the politicians is a peculiarly happy one—so it is, *for the politicians.* But the system makes school terms shorter and shorter; a poorer class of teachers, because of diminished salaries, and of course a continually lowered standard of education. Finally, Mr. Chairman, we who are disfranchised, anxious to become Americans in all things, wish to impress on you the fact that any political distinction between people living in the same community which sets a public mark on one man and not on another is sure to create and foster a feeling of caste. Those whom circumstances have made observant see this in the school, in the church, and in social life. Matthew Arnold, in writing of a civilization older than that of Rhode Island and of New England, says that caste barbarizes the upper, vulgarizes the middle, and brutalizes the lower classes. I conclude my remarks by thanking you for the courteous attention you have given me.

Mr. EVANS, of Providence,

the next speaker, did not think it strange that in thirty-five years we should have outgrown the present constitution and need to have it revised. We have trebled the business of the State and the population has about doubled. We are progressing and we want to keep abreast of the times. An extension of suffrage would promote harmony in the community and would be for the best interests of the people and State. The property qualification is an unwise discrimination, and if we look back forty years we will find that the interests of the State have been jeopardized more from above than below. The system by which registry taxes has been paid and then electing to office, whether fit for it or not, the man who paid the taxes, has not done us any credit any way. He was, he said, in favor of equality before the law.

Mr. Lapham—Would you extend the right of suffrage to women?

Mr. Evans—I am in favor of women voting; 1 don't want to pledge you to it. The best law is to have all work together, and it would be for the best interests of the State to have the constitution revised. We should keep in harmony with the people of other States.

Col. JAMES MORAN, of Providence,

said he was interested in the question of giving the ballot to naturalized citizens, and particularly to the soldiers who had fought the battles of the Union. He had been a soldier, had held a commission from the State, and for the past twenty years he had not been thought worthy of the ballot, and he could not exercise the right of suffrage without conforming to a degrading qualification. Since he returned from the war he had seen men who had come within the lines of the Union forces exercise this privilege of voting while he himself could not do it because he was not born in this country. He was not opposed to the "contrabands" voting, but merely cited the matter as an illustration of how unjustly this property qualification operates. It affected many others as it did himself. They fought to make the slave a freeman; they succeeded; the slave has become a voter and yet the soldiers who did this are not allowed to vote in Rhode Island. He did not believe a majority of the people were opposed to granting this privilege. He hoped a constitutional convention would be called. No one generation under a Republican form of government has a right to bind a future generation so that no generation thereafter can change the fundamental law.

Reference has been made from time to time to the promises made to citizens of foreign birth who enlisted as soldiers, that they would be given the franchise and put on an equality with native citizens. In 1861, two or three days after the first battle of Bull Run, there was a large meeting on Market Square; three or four platforms were erected, and when the speakers appealed to the men of foreign birth to enlist they were told in the name of the State that the franchise would be given them. I heard that promise made, said Col. Moran, and that promise has been unfulfilled for twenty years. It was at a public meeting, and the promise was made by representatives of the State government; all the authority in the State authorized the promise, and it was the means of making hundreds, nay thousands, of citizens of foreign birth go into the army. I did, and I know of many others who did. What was the result? More than one-quarter of the soldiers who enlisted from this State and served the government faithfully were men of foreign birth. I am understating rather than overstating the fact. There were 24,000 men credited to the State, and of these between six and seven thousand were men of foreign birth. Another thing, these men enlisted for three years, and generally served the term, too. They were not three months' men or nine months' men, so that making a proper ratio of the number that served the State and the length of time that they served, the number of years served by men of foreign birth was as one to three—that at least one-third of the quota were men of foreign birth and served the State an equal number of years that two thirds of native soldiers did. He had given this matter some attention, and examined closely the Adjutant General's report issued under the authority of the State in 1866, and he took his estimates from that report. His estimate was, he believed, an understatement of the fact, as the report was defective in that it did not give the place of birth, but the residence. He was safe, however, in saying that six or seven thousand men entered the army in Rhode Island regiments in addition to many who enlisted in regiments in other States. And these men are deprived of the right of suffrage. It will be a stigma upon the State until it is removed. The State says he is not fit to have the suffrage, while nearly twenty years ago he was deemed fit enough to have a commission and command a company.

Another view of the matter was that Rhode Island by its attitude on the 15th Amendment forced a more objectionable suffrage on other States than can possibly be brought about by any changes in our constitution, for the men of foreign birth who would become entitled to vote are fully as intelligent as the natives. Why do you make a sand bank the criterion of a man's qualification? There are men who don't know A, B, C, and yet have voted for years because they own $134 worth of real estate. His individual opinion was that if a constitutional convention is not called, that at least an amendment should be recommended giving naturalized citizens the right to vote, especially the soldiers who fought for the country. He thought the claims of women should be considered, too. He believed they were as capable of exercising the right as intelligently as men, and that they would not be influenced by the same mercenary motives that men have. He concluded his speech by relating an incident that occurred in the Third Ward, showing that a storekeeper voted for twenty-five cents.

Senator Dyer, of Johnston, asked what was the nationality of this man?

Col. Moran—He was a native American, sir; "dyed in the wool;" I don't know but he traces his ancestry to Plymouth Rock. I claim that if the suffrage was extended there would not be the same corruption of voters; people wouldn't have money enough to go around.

Mr. Sheffield—Would it not be only widening the field?

Col. Moran—It would cost more than they could pay. There are not many men now who can say they hold the State in their breast pocket; not as many as there used to be. But I can say that if a constitutional convention were called and these questions were properly discussed and placed before the people without prejudice, the State would be benefited a thousandfold.

Mr. HENRY TYTAR, of Warwick.

Mr. Chairman and Gentlemen of the Committee:

I am one of the disfranchised in Rhode Island, although being a citizen of the United States and a soldier in the war for the Union. I fought for the national flag at Yorktown, Hanover Court House, Fredericksburg and Chancellorville, besides being in thirty-two lesser engagements and skirmishes. I would willingly go through the same or like dangers and hardships again in defense of the Union flag, if called on to do so by the national or State authorities. Surely, my record is a sufficient guarantee of my loyalty to American institutions. In every other State in the Union my political rights as an American citizen would be recognized. It is left for Rhode Island alone to set a mark on me as one unfit to have any voice in the political affairs of the nation, although, as I have said, I offered life itself on many a hard-fought field in defense of this State and of all the States.

Mr. JAMES H. LEWIS, of Cumberland.

Mr. Chairman and Gentlemen:

In looking over the columns of a weekly newspaper printed here in Rhode Island, I found the editor to say that other States have revised their constitutions because they were poor, while the constitution of this State is so good that it needs no alteration.

Yes, Mr. Chairman, our constitution is so "good" that it deprives thirty or forty thousand of our so-called citizens from helping to make the officers of the State and of the United States, while thousands of its foreign-born property-holders refuse to qualify themselves through such means as it prescribes. Are not the learned divines of the State, who have been born in foreign lands, intelligent enough to be worthy of some consideration?

The gentleman who preceded me, Col. Moran, in speaking of the soldiers and sailors, brought to mind a case that came under my own observation while circulating one of these petitions. The father of a family went to the war in 1861, was killed by a rebel bullet, and his bones are bleaching on southern soil to-day. His two sons also went to the war in 1862, and fought to its close in '65, when they returned home to comfort that mother, who had lost a fond husband, and to take his place in attending to the household wants. They were good enough to face rebel fire, but they are not good enough to have a voice in the politics of Rhode Island, because they were born in a foreign land.

Again, the foreigner, when leaving home and turning his face towards the western republic says, when he bids his friends good-bye, that he is going to that land where all men are equal. He can go to any other State and that motto prevails, but here in Rhode Island he finds that he has to buy $134 worth of sand before he is the equal of his fellow-man. For these and hundreds of other reasons, you should report back to the House favorably our petition for the calling of a constitutional convention; as gentlemen of good understanding, I hope you will do this justice.

MR. CALEB WESTCOTT, OF WARWICK.

Mr. Chairman and Gentlemen of the Committee:

There is one thing which should be abolished from our State constitution, for the reason that it makes a portion of our citizens mere machines, so to speak. I refer now to the registry tax. And if any person will be interested enough to examine any of the books at the town or city clerks' offices, I think they will find that nine-tenths of all the names are registered within a very few days of the end of December, the last month in which a citizen can register his name in order to become a registry voter for the coming political year. Now why is this so? Why do they wait until the last moment? It does not cost anything to register their names. I think it can be answered in this way. The constitution when first adopted allowed any man to have the names of as many as he saw fit to be registered. The men themselves knew no more about it than though they were machines. The politicians made up their list of names of those who were of their political stripe, and when the time for the payment of the tax came around the politicians paid the tax—almost every dollar of it—and when election day came nearly all of these men were carried to the polls, and how do you suppose they voted? Like intelligent voters, men who had been assessed a tax, men who had helped to contribute to the support of the government under which they lived, like freemen, like men? I think not, but as slaves, as machines, merely doing what their masters intended they should do when they registered their names for them. And, Mr. Chairman, is it much better now under the present law? In fact, is it any better? Let us examine for a moment how it works under the law as it now is. Mr. A. is a politician, a leader, a wire-puller in his party. He takes the trouble to go, at about the last days of registering, and drum up those who have not registered, (and I will be bound to say that three-quarters of them would not register if they were not urged to do so by his telling them they ought to go and attend to it, and in many instances furnishes conveyances for them to the place of registry. Now he calls upon and urges them that he knows to be friendly to his party. Those that are of the opposite political faith he cares not for. In fact, he had rather they would not register; he only wants those that will help him. Now I ask does this state of affairs make of men what they should be? Does it make men, intelligent men, of them? I think you will agree with me when I say that it does not, but that it degrades, and has a strong tendency to make mere machines of them. Now I say, do away with this registry tax and assess every man a poll tax. Give him to understand that he is a part of the governed; that the laws are made for his especial benefit and protection; that he is by those laws protected in his life and property, and the liberty that he has, the privileges he enjoys, are his by right; that he is one of the people that make our town, State and nation, and as such is bound to help maintain and support the laws wherever he lives, and that he by paying his tax does so support the government, and have him to know that he does not pay his tax for the privilege of voting. He should be compelled to pay his tax, his proportion, towards the support of the government, and under certain restrictions or qualifications should have the franchise; should have a voice in who should make our laws and who should be our rulers. In this way, Mr. Chairman and Gentlemen of the Committee, and I know of no better way, a man can be made to feel that he is a man, that he is a freeman, and that he is an American citizen.

And, Mr. Chairman, in closing I will say a word about the property qualification. I am in favor of doing away with it entirely. I claim it to be unjust. Take it in our cities and large towns, where is a man, or how is he to buy one or two hundred dollars worth of real estate? Perhaps the State might now sell him a lot in the tract they have just bought of the Charlestown Indians, and then he could vote on a certificate procured ten days before each general election. I am in favor of giving the ballot to every man who is a citizen and pays a tax, whether on real or personal property or poll tax, believing that taxation without representation is not the right form of a Republican government.

Mr. LOUIS KRANZ, of Providence,

said he was not an intruder in the State, but had come here by invitation of a manufacturing concern; had been a citizen of the United States years ago, and cast his first vote for Lincoln in 1860; had sat on juries in Brooklyn, N. Y., for four years. On coming here in 1876 was surprised to find himself deprived of the rights of citizenship, such as he had enjoyed in several States of the Union; felt as if he had come outside of the United States. He believed the people of Rhode Island had a superstitious reverence for the soil of their State, shown in adhering to this property qualification as regards the votes of foreigners. He would remind the people that the soil of Rhode Island has as much to do with the greatness of the State as it has with the greatness of the now celebrated Yazoo County, in Mississippi. It was not the soil, but the men of brains and of skilled and industrious hands, which made any State great and prosperous.

The greatest hindrance to the prosperity of a State are those who own real estate and let it lie idle. Voting ought also to be free from any tax. It would be good if people realized that all taxes have to be earned first by productive labor before the so-called taxpayer is able to pay them. All taxes are a necessary evil. And it was not the height of statemanship how to raise taxes, but how to get along with as little as possible. He did not object to an educational qualification, but although his hair was getting gray, he would, if necessary, go to school again. He concluded by feeling disgraced that a small amount of real estate should outweigh intelligence, character and manhood—took comfort in the thought that our common fatherland is large and Rhode Island small and easy to get away from.

P. J. McCARTHY, Esq., of Providence,

favored a poll tax instead of a registry law, and referred feelingly to the claims of naturalized citizens, he himself having been a voter but now disfranchised.

At the third hearing, which occurred on the evening of February 21st, nine more of the petitioners had opportunity to present their case. Owing to the lateness of the hour and the necessarily limited number of the hearings, several who were present and desirous of speaking were unable to do so.

The first gentleman to appear in behalf of the petitioners was

Mr. C. C. HEINTZEMAN, of Providence,

who said he was a disfranchised citizen and felt deeply the injustice of the laws of this State.

"I am," he said, "a native of Germany, and came to this country when quite young. I served in the army from May, 1861, to 1864; took an active part with the Republican party in Maryland; went to Massachusetts, and there found my rights as a soldier and citizen recognized; but, about three years ago, I came to Rhode Island, and was surprised to find that I could not vote even for President of the United States. Of course I cannot buy a piece of property in the city for $134. Thinking of Republican principles, and thinking of the founder of the State, Roger Williams, I thought it was strange that just here there should be such a restriction, and it seemed impossible that any man could affirm that it is justifiable."

Germans, when they came to this country, were Republicans. They
were always on the right side, and they worked for such candidates as
were an honor to the country. The Germans were not very numerous,
but there was a number of them disfranchised. The law was hard on
them. All through the West Germans could vote, and those who were
here, a majority of them, were intelligent. They felt the injustice of the
law, and he felt that, as having served the country and served his party, it
was unjust to require him to possess real estate to entitle him to vote. He
knew of Germans who had voted against amending the constitution in
several cases, having themselves gained a little property; but he also knew
how these men had got their property, and what was their standard of intelligence. In three or four cases they were of the worst types.

Mr. JOHN FRANCIS SMITH, of Oaklawn,

said that a good deal of time had been taken up with the question as to
the power of the General Assembly to call a convention. He appre-
hended that the difficulty was not so much a question of methods as to the
thing itself. The people are desirous that certain changes shall be incorporated into the law, but are not so particular how it shall be done. The
speaker then went on to argue that the present position of the State of
Rhode Island, in regard to the rights of its citizens, was as much of a
nullification of the laws of the general government as South Carolina
ever attempted. The present partial suffrage degraded the individual.
It has been assumed that the possession of real estate makes men more
patriotic. Was that true? How many of those who went forth to the
war from this State were holders of real estate? This seemed to be an
overlooking of certain facts. It seemed to affirm that property is the basis
of taxation. This, in the opinion of the speaker, was a fallacious idea,
for taxes, as the last resort, are almost wholly based on labor. The patriots of the revolution had said that taxation without representation was
tyranny. Was it any less tyranny in 1881 than in 1776? It has just been
stated in the United States Senate that a republic is not necessarily a
democracy. How, then, he would like to ask, does it differ from an
oligarchy?

It has been said that the people of this State have already voted against
an extension of suffrage. Was that true? A part of the people enjoying
special immunities and privileges have merely refused to extend the same
advantages to others.

The speaker next touched upon the question of corruption in politics,
and considered the present registry system a prolific source of such corruption.

It has been asserted in Congress that the way Rhode Island manages her
affairs is no concern of the people of the other States. It seemed to the
speaker, however, that the people of every State have a right to protest

against the injustice in any State. Rhode Island was an earnest supporter of the last three amendments to the United States constitution, which was certainly a meddling with the internal affairs of other States. Her position was one favoring exclusion here, and inclusion in other States. The speaker did not understand that sympathy was bounded by State lines. The Senate of Rhode Island had just asserted its sympathy for the sufferers of Ireland, and the people of other States had certainly a right to object to the wrongs done by Rhode Island to her own citizens

Hon. GEORGE L. CLARKE, of Providence,

did not believe that the fundamental law should be changed for any light reason or in haste, and he believed that what had worked well in practice, protecting property and the rights of citizens, should be allowed to continue. On the other hand, he did not believe that because a law was old or had existed from time immemorial, that, therefore, under altered circumstances and conditions, the fundamental law should be held forever inviolable, and never be altered or amended, to meet the progressive necessities of those who live under it. The present constitution had been adopted about forty years ago, and since that time the State had largely increased in population, its industries had become diversified, and the conditions and circumstances having been changed, it was reasonable to suppose that a change was necessary in the fundamental law.

If the right to call a constitutional convention did not exist, it was useless to hold the meetings of the committee. If it was held that the constitution could be amended only by a vote of three-fifths of the people voting, the present constitution may be considered as fixed for all time, as a minority of the people, as we are now situated, could forever prevent any change. Notably was this illustrated only a few years ago, when an attempt was made to amend the constitution so as to allow naturalized citizens who had served in the war and been honorably discharged the right to vote. The amendment was voted for by a majority, but failed to receive the three-fifths necessary to its adoption.

It would seem, said Mr. Clarke, that he whose love for the institutions under which he lives is such that he is willing to brave the dangers of battle, to risk his life through long and weary campaigns in their defence, is entitled, if anybody is, to have a voice in the government under which he lives. In ancient times it was held that *only* he who bore arms in defence of the State should have a voice in its government, but we seem to have improved on those ancient barbarians, as we call them, and we decree that he who takes his life in his hands and perils it, that the nation may live, shall have the glorious privilege of *standing one side*, and beholding those whom he has bravely defended exercising all those rights of citizenship which he has faced death to preserve or acquire.

And I will venture to predict, said Mr. Clarke, that our present constitution can *never* be amended, in any important particular, or when any desirable change is required, under Article 13 of our present constitution, requiring a three-fifths vote.

The law authorizing the calling of the convention which made the present constitution provided that, if adopted by the majority of the people voting, the constitution should be the supreme law; so, in this connection, it was pertinent to ask what right a majority at that time had to tie for all time the hands of those who came after.

It is generally conceded as good American doctrine, that what a majority can do, a majority can undo—what a majority can establish, a majority can set aside. This seems to me nothing more than ordinary common sense.

Mr. Sheffield—Some of the most eminent lawyers in this country have decided that that is wrong. You think Judge Shaw is a good judge?

Mr. Clarke—Yes, sir; but the practical question before us is, if the majority of the people voting could require three-fifths to amend the constitution, the conclusion is logically irresistible that the same majority could require four-fifths, or seven-eighths, or the *whole* people, to vote in favor of any amendment before it could be adopted. So that a single individual voter could, on this theory, prevent for all time the adoption of any amendment whatever.

We can all see the perfect absurdity of an argument running in this direction.

Mr. Lapham—What is there unreasonable in requiring that three out of five people should vote to change a law?

Mr. Clarke—While it is true that all changes in the fundamental law should be deliberately made, yet it is seldom that you can get a three-fifths vote for anything, and by this rule it would be next to impossible to change the constitution in any material point.

Quoting the sections of the constitution bearing upon the matter in discussion, Mr. Clarke asked: " Is there anywhere a prohibition against calling a constitutional convention?"

Mr. Sheffield—I think so, by necessary implication.

Mr. Clarke—I should say only by implication; but not by " necessary implication."

Mr. Sheffield—By necessary implication I should say—by all the rules of construction.

Mr. Clarke—Do you find it in Article 13 of the constitution?

Mr. Sheffield—Yes.

Mr. Clarke—That hardly strikes my mind as a prohibition. It simply says that the General Assembly may prepare amendments, but it no where prohibits the people themselves under the proper forms of law from forming a new constitution whenever they desire to do so. On the other hand, the right of the people to make or alter their constitutions of government is given in almost express terms in Section 1 of Article 1 of our present constitution, and the right of the General Assembly to call a convention to form a new constitution is found in Section 10 of Article 4, under which the Assembly may at any time call a convention for the above purpose.

Mr. Lapham—Do you suppose it was the intention that a convention should be called every two or three years?

Mr. Clarke—I suppose that the *power* is there.

Mr. Lapham—Read it altogether. Would you infer that that was the intention?

Mr. Clarke—I see no reason why that is not a legitimate construction, and I think that the only safeguard against this calling of a convention would be the general intelligence of the people. It is never wise for the party in power to disregard the reasonable demands of the people. If there is any general wish for a change, it is sure to come. By gracefully yielding to this demand, we make the very people who may be now our political enemies our political friends.

Mr. Lapham—I don't think it is a question of who shall be in power. It is of right and justice.

Mr. Clarke—I have found that the question of right and justice may be sometimes governed by party feelings.

Mr. Lapham—I don't know what effect this will have on others, but, so far as losing power is concerned, it will have no effect on me.

Mr. Sheffield—I hardly think that is proper for consideration. We have tried to do our duty.

Mr. Clarke—I am saying it as a matter of fact, and not in any sense as a threat. These provisions in regard to voting are among the most important in our constitution; the right of the citizen to vote is the basis—

Mr. Sheffield—Do you think voting a trust or inherent right?

Mr. Clarke—I think there are very few inherent rights, but I think the right to vote is a much a right as the right to be governed by a majority, and that it is for the interest of the State that every person having an interest in the State should have a voice in the government.

Mr. Sheffield—He should have intelligence to know what is for the interest of the State, and integrity and courage to do it."

Mr. Clarke—If we have a fair vote and an honest count—no bribery and corruption—we need not fear. If we had an educational test, and if it could be applied to all alike, it might be desirable; but the whole registry tax system has been a great source of bribery and corruption. I think every gentleman on the committee has seen it.

Mr. Lapham—Suppose that was abolished, would not other means be equally open to corruption, as in Philadelphia and New York?

Mr. Clarke—I am not so utopian as to believe that we can make all people honest or virtuous by law. So long as people are ready to buy votes there will probably be other people ready to sell them. Bribery will doubtless continue so long as other evils in this world continue.

Mr. Lapham—Then, if we do what is asked, we only change the mode of doing?

Mr. Clarke—My objection is that, by continuing the registry tax system, you tend to promote corruption. We cannot get rid of an evil by laws, but we need not promote it. I don't believe, as a fact, you will find more corruption among one class of voters than among another. The State should not frame laws to promote it.

Mr. Lapham—When we provide that a naturalized citizen shall not be allowed to vote unless he owns $134 worth of real estate, haven't we provided for a class who will not sell their votes?

Mr. Clarke—Not necessarily, by any means. I have known people who were worth much more than $134 to sell their votes. It is true generally that the more small holdings of real estate in the community the better and safer it is.

Mr. Lapham—Now would it be wiser to give the right of voting to naturalized citizens, or say that native citizens should own $134 worth of real estate?

Mr. Clarke—I doubt if you can have the government even tolerably free from corruption so long as voting is in any direct way dependent upon tax paying. Voting and tax paying should be entirely divorced from each other.

The government should tax all its citizens in proportion to their ability to bear its burdens. It has the power to collect its taxes, and can enforce their collection in such manner as it deems proper; but the right to vote ought never to depend upon the voluntary payment of any tax. So sure as this is done corruption in elections is sure to follow.

Mr. Clarke continued his remarks by enumerating other desirable changes that might be made. Among other things he alluded to the tenure of the Judges of the Supreme Court as a matter of high importance. At present all the Judges of the Supreme Court can be turned out of office at any May Session of the General Assembly. In his view the Judges should be appointed for life, subject only to removal by impeachment. The bench would then be independent of political or party action. As the matter now stands it might be in the power of any party that felt aggrieved by some decision of the court to cause its removal for political reasons. This danger to the position of the judiciary of the State ought not to remain.

Mr. Clarke concluded his remarks by enumerating other desirable changes that might be made, and thanking the committee for their attention, took his seat.

Mr. FREDERIC A. HINCKLEY, OF PROVIDENCE.

Mr. Chairman and Gentlemen of the Committee:

I am one of the signers of the petition for a constitutional convention, and I gladly appear here to further identify myself with this movement. To my mind there are two questions involved:

First—Have the people a right to meet in constitutional convention to revise their old constitution or adopt a new one,

Second—If the right exists are there good and sufficient reasons for its exercise?

On the first of these points I cannot of course speak as a lawyer, but only from such understanding of our theory of government as comes from a long and careful study of its fundamental principles. The framers and ratifiers of our Rhode Island constitution decreed that a three-fifths vote of the electors voting should be necessary to amend it. It is generally conceded here to-night by the committee, as well as by ourselves, that the right to require a three-*fifths* vote implies the right to require a three-*fourths*, a *seven-eighths*, or even a *unanimous* vote. So that had our fathers chosen to have required a unanimous vote of the electors voting they could have done so, and according to the present view, that the people may not meet in their sovereign capacity and make a new constitution if they choose so to do, from that decision of the fathers there would have been no appeal. So that at any time had this unanimous ratification of an amendment been required, one elector could have defeated all changes in our constitution and we should have had in Rhode Island what? Not the government of the people, not the government of the electors, or a majority of the electors even, but the government of one man—an oligarchy. I confess, gentlemen, I shrink from any such conclusion. I do not believe the American principle rests upon so weak a foundation, and I believe, therefore, that the assumption which makes its complete overthrow in logic possible, must in itself be a fallacy. Without troubling the authorities, which have been wisely and fully quoted to you by others, this seems to me the simple common sense of the case.

Now what reasons are there why a constitutional convention of the people should be held? The chief reason in my judgment is the great difficulty of amending the constitution through the ordinary channel. By the terms of our organic law, a large number of citizens are, in violation of our fundamental principle of government, disfranchised, and a three-fifths vote of those exercising the suffrage is required. The practical result is, as you all know, that there is a peculiar and all but insurmountable prejudice in Rhode Island against alterations in the constitution. Now, sir, I believe that prejudice to be a most harmful thing. Ideas of government grow, practical methods of government should grow also. It ought to be our constant aim to lift our form of administration to the level of the highest interpretation of the democratic principle. Our fathers rebelled against the arbitrary power of one man. They set their faces toward the logical antithesis of kingly rule, the government of every man by himself. But recognizing, as we must all recognize that, as a dream of the millenium, they tried as practical men to approach as near to the ideal as possible, in a government of all the people, by all the people, for all the people. A government of consent—that was their theory. It is true they did not fully apply it, but the efforts of the nation for the last hundred years have been towards its fullest possible application.

Now I claim that we in Rhode Island are not outside the influence of this progress. The demand for the abolition of the property qualification, the demand for woman suffrage, the demand for a more equitable representation of the city of Providence in the General Assembly, are but illustrations of the growth in our midst of the democratic idea. I do not believe in the policy of obstruction. I do not fear the results of agitation. It is more than safe, it is eminently wise, expedient and just, that we should summon the best thought and experience of the State to meet in constitutional convention to consider these various demands and all others which may be introduced. Let them come, I care not how many, for candid examination and settlement. It is not a measure of rebellion. It is simply a measure of peaceful revolution, recognizing the people as the sovereign power. I am heartily in sympathy with all the purposes of the petitioners. I believe they point to a happy way of reconciling interests at present becoming more and more antagonistic, and therefore I hope our prayer may be granted.

Mr. CHARLES P. ADAMS, of Pawtucket,

said that in the late general election the vote of Rhode Island was one to ten of the population, while in other States it ranged from one to five to one to four. Throughout the whole country the ratio was about one to five and a half. He thought that, if the laws in our statute book need amending and changing every year, the constitution, which is only a more fundamental law, needs revision at the end of forty years. This speaker went on to criticise Senator Anthony's recent speech, and argue that the State should not cling to antiquated methods when it had outgrown them.

Mr. D. D. DONOVAN, of Providence.

Mr. Chairman and Gentlemen of the Committee:

As one of the petitioners to the General Assembly for a constitutional convention to revise the constitution of this State, I appear before you for the purpose of stating briefly the reasons that actuated me in signing that petition. Though the petitioners asked for and desired that a special committee should be appointed to consider the need of such a revision of the present constitution as would make it conform to the wants of the people, I can say for myself, and I think that I speak the sentiments of most of those interested in the movement, that we have no fault to find with the manner in which we have been treated by this committee. I have attended all the hearings you have held in reference to it, and I believe that your committee are actuated with a desire to remedy the evils we complain of, though you may not all agree as to the means whereby to reach the desired end.

Now, Mr. Chairman, it is not my purpose to take up your time by entering into a discussion of the power of the General Assembly, or of the power of the people through their representatives, to call a convention for the purpose of revising the constitution of this State. That question has been ably presented by gentlemen who were qualified for the task. But I will ask your attention for a few moments to the reasons why such a convention should be called.

The first and greatest reason is that the present constitution disfranchises a large number of the citizens of the United States, who, in any other State in the Union, would be entitled to the right of suffrage. It is impossible to get at the exact number, but it has been variously estimated at from five to ten thousand. It has been stated in the Senate of the United States by the honorable gentleman (Senator Anthony) that represents this State in the councils of the nation that there are but two thousand and sixty citizens of the United States disfranchised by the present constitution through the property qualification. This may be true, but, sir, he fails to state how many would become citizens were this disqualification removed. What inducement is there for a man to swear allegiance to a government that fails to protect him in one of the dearest rights of citizenship, the right to vote? I will state right here that it is my firm conviction that those two thousand and sixty spoken of are composed of persons who were citizens of other States before removal here, or were property owners in this State, but through the vicissitudes of fortune came under the disqualifying clause of the constitution. Quite a number of the latter class have appeared before you and pointed out to you the injustice it works in their case.

I am one of a large number that come under the former, having been a citizen of the neighboring State of Connecticut, voting there for about twelve years, enjoying all the privileges of citizenship. I come to your State voluntarily, and contribute by my labor to build up your industries and to so educate my children that they may become useful members of society. Now what do you offer me in return? You say the protection of your laws, with the proviso that you reserve to yourself the right to make the law.

Is this a fair exchange? I give you in time of peace the labor of my hands, for the great source of the wealth of your State is labor. In time of war, at the command of the nation, whose constitution I have sworn to support, my life stands between your institutions and those who would seek to subvert them, and yet the honorable Senator before alluded to tells me that I came here uninvited, and can go when I please. That I came uninvited is true. But, sir, I *was* invited to stay and contribute by the humble abilities that I may possess to develop the industries of this Commonwealth.

Mr. Sheffield objected to any criticisms of Senator Anthony, for the reason that he was not present to defend himself.

Mr. Chairman, I have only to say that the honorable senator's speech has gone forth to the country through the public press, and we, the people whom it is intended to affect, in my opinion, have a right to take exceptions to the arguments therein set forth.

There is another phase of this question that has engaged a good deal of attention during the hearings before this committee, and that is the registry laws. The ablest minds in the State have been grappling for years with the problem, how to purify the elections, and it is an acknowledged fact that so far they have failed. Then the question arises, What is the cause, and where is the remedy? In my opinion, gentlemen, the primary cause is, that you put a price upon the ballot, and you never can remedy the evil so long as you retain that great source of corruption in your political system. You will pardon me for calling your attention for a moment to the registry system of Connecticut, which I confidently believe is one of the best of any State in the Union. There the matter of taxation is entirely separated from the ballot. Every male citizen over twenty-one years of age is obliged to pay a tax of two dollars a year, unless excused by reason of being a member of the State militia, and the money derived from this source is used to support the military system of the State, while every male citizen of the United States twenty-one years of age, who has resided in the State one year, and in the town where he makes his application six months, and is able to read, is entitled to vote.

The election law adopted by the Legislature in 1877 provides that each town shall choose at its annual election two registrars of voters, and the two persons having the highest number of votes are the ones to be declared elected; but no person can vote for more than one registrar, so that both parties are always represented, and in this way fairness of registration is secured. The principal duties of registrars is to make out a correct list or all voters in their respective towns at least eighteen days before the day of election, appoint a moderator and box-tender, whose duties are similar to those of the warden and clerk in this State.

By Mr. Sheffield—Is it not charged that there is a great deal of corruption in Connecticut under this system?

Mr. Chairman, that there is corruption in elections everywhere, I don't pretend to deny, but, sir, in Connecticut, it is in spite of the law, while in Rhode Island the law creates the opportunity for it. I know something about the politics of Connecticut, having been an active member of the Republican party in the ward where I resided, and I will say this, that I never saw a vote purchased; but there is what is called a floating vote, which in many cases can be secured by the use of money. It is composed of a class of men without principle, who will work all the day of election distributing tickets, or looking after voters, for the sum of from two to five dollars, and these men are mostly secured by the party they are supposed to belong to, for fear they would vote for the other. In Hartford, with a voting population of from 8,000 to 10,000 I should not estimate this class at over 300.

It has been claimed that the restriction on the suffrage in this State is no greater than the educational test in Connecticut. Let us see how the figures will bear out the claim. At the last Presidential election this State, with a population of 276,000, cast a vote of about 29,000. In Connecticut, where the population is a little over 600,000, the vote at the same election was over 130,000. Hartford, with 40,000 inhabitants, cast as large a vote as Providence, with 100,000. These are the figures, gentlemen. You can draw your own conclusions.

Mr. Chairman, I have occupied your time longer than I had intended, and in conclusion, let me hope that you will take seriously into consideration the grievances we complain of, for grievances they are. Let me ask you where is the justice of admitting to the elective franchise my neighbor, who occupies the same position in life I do, for the sum of $1, while to me you fix the price at $134, and it amounts to just that, for where can I purchase a piece of land for $134 that will be of any other use than to vote on. By adhering to this obnoxious system you lose the services of the best element of the naturalized citizens, for no man imbued with the spirit of American freedom will consent to accept the privilege of voting under such conditions. I would rather forever continue protesting against its injustice than for one moment accept the privilege of voting under your present constitution.

Mr. HENRY APPLETON, of Providence,

stated that there were many prominent signers of the petition for a constitutional convention who did not attend the hearing, and that the movement represented all political opinions and the wishes of people in all conditions of life.

Mr. ALEXANDER BROWN, of Providence,

favored extending the franchise to every man who complies with the constitutional requirements of the nation. Immigrants, when entitled to all the rights of citizenship, feel an increased interest in their adopted country. To withhold this right tends to the injury of the individual, and is contrary to the golden rule. He appealed to the common sense of the whole country, east, west, north and south, to decide in this matter.

He said: When our whole country was bleeding at every pore, and the hearts of nearly all began to give way, when, after the battle of Antietam, men could not be induced, nor bought, nor bribed to go to the front, when the 11th and 12th Rhode Island regiments lay for over six months upon the training ground unfilled, just at that time I felt and saw it my duty to offer myself in defense of my adopted country. So I put on the blue, against the protest of my partner in business, and also of my wife whom I left with four little ones to be provided for by charity in case I fell, (as many a noble fellow did,) but go was the word. The next morning after I enlisted twelve out of the fourteen men employed by the firm of J. & A.

Brown did the same. My partner, left without help, was unable to do the work, so that when I returned the business was so injured that we could not rally it. We were obliged to fail, the real estate upon which I had voted, always the Republican ticket, going with the rest of the property, and carrying with it in this State my vote. Where is the consistency of this state of things? Can it be made to chime with the genius of this Republic? Now look at it for a few minutes. The colored men of the South, the property of the white planters, who were made free by a war measure of our noble President, can come to this State, register their names and by the payment of one dollar can vote—no questions asked; but I, who have sacrificed all that gives me a show here, cannot vote. Oh! Rhode Island, the boasted State of equal rights for all, where is your consistency! I don't find fault that my colored brethren have this right, for it is a right; but how about me and others like me?

I have read an able article in the Providence Journal, called "Defense of Rhode Island," from the pen of Senator Anthony, and all that I have to say concerning it is that I have read just as able articles in defence of chattle slavery.

Dr. GARVIN'S ADDRESS.

When the State House of Representatives denied to the petitioners for a constitutional convention the desired special committee, I shared with others the feeling that the reference to the judiciary committee lessened our prospects of success. But with the progress of these hearings, that sense of disappointment has changed to one of satisfaction, not only in consequence of the great courtesy and attention which has been paid to our wishes by every member of your committee, but also because a strong and just cause fares best at the hands of those most qualified by intellectual training and professional pursuits to judge of its merits. What we have to fear is prejudice, not merely conservatism in a proper sense of that term, but a stupid conservatism which ignores reason, and like the Bourbon, fixing its gaze exclusively upon the past, disregards the claims of the present and the future.

The legal question involved in the calling of a constitutional convention needs no further elucidation than it has already received at these hearings. I would simply say that Rhode Island is unfortunate, indeed, if, of all the thirty-eight States in the Union, she alone is debarred from revising her constitution. Were that view of the case accepted, the 6,973 votes which fixed the arbitrary number of three-fifths as the proportion of the popular vote required to amend could as well have said four-fifths, —or even five-fifths, and thus have prevented the teeming population of to-day and of all the future from altering a single word or letter of their fundamental law. If this be not a *reductio ad absurdum*, where can one be found? We may, therefore, expect that, admitting the authority of the

General Assembly to provide for the calling of a convention, your report will be directed to the expediency of such legislative action.

Without repeating the various arguments which have been adduced already, and which are fresh in your memory, I venture to name a few reasons why it seems proper that you should favor the wishes of the petitioners. The fundamental, and indeed all-sufficient reason, is that justice may be done. Hamilton in the Federalist unequivocally says: "Justice is the end of government. It is the end of civil society." If this be true, and if, as has been repeatedly asserted in your hearing, a crying injustice is laid by the State constitution upon a large portion of our fellow-citizens, is it not incumbent upon the General Assembly in the most direct and speedy manner, now when its attention is called to the subject, to act in the interest of justice? United States citizens subject to the same burdens of indirect taxation and military duty, contributing equally to the growth and prosperity of the State, are disfranchised by an inequitable provision of the constitution.

At the first hearing, I stated, upon the authority of Mr. Carl Ernst, that there were probably in Rhode Island 10,000 disfranchised citizens of the United States. The estimate, or guess I think it must have been, seemed, and has now been shown to be too large. Senator Anthony gives the number, as taken from the census of 1870, at 2,060. This reduction shows two things: First, that the migration of persons of foreign birth from other States to this is not so large as has been supposed, and with an extended suffrage not sufficient, as has been feared, to have any dangerous influence in our elections; and, secondly, what an effectual bar the real estate qualification is to the naturalization and consequent identification of resident foreigners with our institutions.

The claim is made that exact justice demands equal suffrage for women as well as men of foreign birth. If so, as I do not deny, that is an additional reason for holding a convention; but I call the attention of the committee to this important difference between the two contrasted pleas for political equity. Women generally do not wish for the right to vote, so, with some plausibility, it is argued, that their exclusion from the suffrage is the result of a mutual agreement between the sexes. Not so with the males. To a man, they ardently desire the franchise, and keenly feel the brand of inferiority which this State alone sets upon them.

Not only as an act of justice, but also to support our character for consistency, should equal suffrage be granted. Inconsistency between the words and the acts of an individual indicates a lack either of intellectual or will power. Every educated man is under bonds to himself and to society to abstain from saying one thing and doing the opposite. Practice must go with preaching in order that the latter may be effectual.

Two or three months ago I had the pleasure to be present at the organization in this city of an association designed to promote equal political rights in the Southern States. As I listened to the reading of the constitution, I endorsed every word of it, and would gladly have affixed my signature had it not been for one thing. I thought, how can we consistently and successfully ask the Southern whites to confer political rights which we in another manner deny at home. Must we not first pluck the beam out of our own eye before we can see clearly to remove the mote (or beam) from our neighbor's eye? It is true we do not reverse the decision at the polls by gross intimidation of dependent voters, nor by a fraudulent count of the votes cast, but we as effectually prevent the exercise of the right. Indeed, the wrong at the South is in its nature temporary, and with the reorganization of parties, which has already occurred in some States, and is rapidly approaching in others, the legal right which already exists will be assured in practice. But here the deprivation is permanent, rendering the condition of the disfranchised more hopeless.

In comparing our political conditions with that at the South, where my boyhood and youth were passed, I am more and more struck with their similarity. The average white southerner, as Tourgee correctly states in his " Bricks without Straw," likes the negro well enough when " kept in his own place," but as to his right to political equality with himself, he is unable to conceive of such a thing. So, many voters in Rhode Island, particularly among those born in the State, are unable to apply at home a principle whose truth they have ever affirmed. When reproached with the inconsistency, some have pronounced it unfortunate for the country that the negroes were given the ballot; but no one, to my knowledge, has ever said that a real estate or educational qualification should be imposed upon the black man, and not upon the white. A few days ago, when in the State Senate, a resolution of sympathy was passed for an oppressed people beyond the sea, sentiments of compassion were expressed for " every human being on the face of the earth of whatever race or color." The scene, creditable as it was to the hearts of the Senators, gave rise to the hope that some overflow of the abounding charity might be expended upon the needs at home. How callous we are to evils ever present! With the example of every surrounding State, with a baptism of freedom from every famous American—but, enough; gentlemen, it is hard to realize that we stand in liberty-loving New England, in the city of Roger Williams, pleading—not in vain, I trust—for the equal right of all men before the law.

It has been asserted in your presence, by one who has an opportunity to know, that skilled labor is more costly in Rhode Island than in adjacent States. How can it be otherwise? If thinking men are placed under a disqualification which they feel to be such, they must receive extra pay for it. This is a law of political economy. Suppose one only of the Southern States defrauded the blacks of their political rights, do you not think that the intelligent among them would desert her borders for the more hospitable commonwealths? As a matter of fact an exodus to the distance of a thousand miles has there taken place in order to escape from political servitude. We may be assured that mechanics will cross the Massachusetts and Connecticut lines for a much less discrimination. That the real estate qualification is regarded as a serious burden you must be aware from what has been said by men of various nationalities at these hearings. I have been surprised, if you have not, at the extent to which the property requirement is regarded by some of the most intelligent to whom it applies as a stigma. Whether aware of it or not, the State is certainly a loser in its material interests, because of its injustice and illiberality.

If time permitted, I think I could show you that, at the same time that our system of suffrage is making semi-chattels of those who do not vote, it is robbing the voters themselves, especially such as have ambition for office, to an unusual extent, of their manliness and independence. Doubtless your own observation has shown this to you more plainly than could any words of mine.

The senior Senator from this State has recently felt it necessary in the national Congress, at Washington, to enter into a "Defense of Rhode Island." In that able address Mr. Anthony clearly shows that in many respects Rhode Island when she entered the Union, was more liberal in the qualifications for suffrage and eligibility to office than the twelve sister States. That our ancestors were so wise as to make the property qualification small, and to eschew all religious tests is a fact of which we may well be proud. But if it is well to admire virtues in our forefathers, it is far better to exercise them ourselves. The early United States Senators of Rhode Island did not need to defend her against charges of illiberality and injustice preferred by members from other States. "It is not by a servile crawling in the paths of our ancestors, but by following the spirit of their institutions, we most fully show our respect for antiquity." Should the prayer of these petitioners for a constitutional convention be granted, it will be the fault of the delegates, if any future Senator of Rhode Island is required to apologize for her institutions. On the contrary, if such convention does its duty, he will be able to point hither to a government which shall be to the other States a model of serviceableness and equity.

Some who favor, and, of course, all who oppose, the holding of a convention have called the attention of petitioners to the folly of asking for too many reforms. If the present constitution were satisfactory in all but one, or even two, particulars, there might be some question as to the propriety of going to the expense of holding a State convention. But, as you well know, year after year, various amendments are proposed by large and influential numbers of citizens for the consideration of the General Assembly, and others would be presented were there any hope of their passage. The Prohibitionists have for several years been drifting to the conclusion, in this State as elsewhere, that only by means of a provision in the organic law can a fair trial of their tenets be secured. The woman suffragists, too, are dependent for success upon a change in the constitution. Just now you have submitted by a member of the General Assembly an amendment providing for a more equal representation in the Lower House. The friends of all these measures must see that they have a bet-

7

ter prospect of gaining their ends through a revision of the entire constitution than by any other means.

The chairman of this committee has had my most hearty approval of his efforts to prevent corruption in elections, but he certainly cannot be satisfied with the result of his measures. In my opinion the united exertions of all who desire a pure ballot-box will be futile, so long as two clauses of the present constitution (one of them at least not likely to be changed by amendment) remain as they are. In my opinion, with those two alterations effected, it would be perfectly within the power of the General Assembly to do away with corrupt practices in politics to an extent now unapproached in any State in the Union. The first clause to which I refer is the one which says that "no compulsory process shall issue for the collection of any registry tax." That is the essential difference between the registry tax which we now have and the poll-tax which we should have. The poll-tax in Massachusetts and some other States is open to the same objection as our registry tax. Just so long as the payment of a tax is not compulsory, but is only to be paid as a prerequisite of voting, call it by what name you will, it will be a prolific breeder of corruption. Here it forbids any poor man, however worthy, from becoming even a candidate for governor in any contested election. How the malign influence reacts upon those who nominally pay it you too well know.

The second clause to which I refer is the last section of Article VIII., which reads: "In all elections held by the people, under this constitution, a majority of all the electors voting shall be necessary to the election of the persons voted for." Without attempting to show how this provision favors corruption, which time and place forbid, I will only say that it makes impossible the application of those principles of representation by means of which every interest in the State has a voice in proportion to its numbers, and by means of which each voter is led to esteem his vote as above price, and each candidate for office to depend upon other than pecuniary influence or wire-pulling for the attainment of his ambition.

In conclusion, let me say that we feel some confidence that you will grant our petition, because we ask but little. The petitioners do not seek permission to supply Rhode Island with a new constitution; they do not ask you or the General Assembly to give one; nor yet that the convention for whose calling you provide should impose one upon the State. They only pray that the people may be allowed to elect delegates who in convention assembled may consider the propriety of certain changes and make recommendations concerning them back again to the people. Or, if you choose so to put it, we shall be satisfied if you simply submit to the people the question, Shall a constitutional convention be held? Yes, or no? This seems but a slight favor to ask or grant.

Of the careful consideration and candid judgment of the committee upon the merits of the question now before it, the petitioners feel assured; in addition they only request that your report be made at as early a day as your engagements may admit.

This closed the hearings. About the 1st of April, after a delay of nearly six weeks, the Committee on the Judiciary reported back the petitions for a constitutional convention, with the recommendation that the petitioners have leave to withdraw.

On the 20th of April the whole matter was finally disposed of by a call of the House, the vote coming on the resolution introduced by Mr. Prendergast, of Burrillville, as a substitute for the recommendation of the committee. His resolution provided for calling town and ward meetings on the 10th of the succeeding August, to choose delegates equal in number to the representation in the General Assembly, to a convention to be held on the first Monday of November following, to frame a new constitution in whole or in part. Mr. Prendergast supported the resolution with a strong plea, which remains unanswered. It was refused a passage by a vote of 4 yeas to 39 nays, and the petitioners were granted leave to withdraw.

Several forcible writers found a hearing in the newspapers, and two of their communications are here inserted.

On March 10, 1881, the following communication was sent to the Providence Press by Mr. JAMES J. SULLIVAN, of Central Falls:

SOME REASONS WHY THE RIGHT OF SUFFRAGE SHOULD BE EXTENDED.

To the Editor of the Press:

Sir: The following article was originally sent to the Providence Journal for publication, in reply to articles which had appeared in that newspaper; but as it was refused admission to its columns, I would like to avail myself of the Press to give some of my reasons why the right of suffrage should be extended.

In the Journal of February 19, a correspondent, " B.," writes as follows: " Since the last proposed amendments were offered and rejected by the people, what has occurred to render such a course desirable or imperative? Are not our industries prosperous? Is any person or class of persons suffering the iron heel of governmental oppression, or have any reason to complain that their rights are not protected?" There is a class of persons who are not "disappointed office seekers and ambitious and anxious partisans" whose rights are not respected, and who feel Rhode Island's "iron heel" of class distinction in politics. Such being the case, it is

. desirable to change the existing laws so as to have them bear equally upon all. As a class we do not advocate free and unrestricted suffrage—there are qualifications of which every man should become possessed before he is admitted to the rights of franchise—but it is unfair and unjust to demand different qualifications from different citizens. Whatever qualifications are demanded, they ought to be the same for all. If $134 in real estate is the best qualification for a citizen of foreign birth, and it is demanded of him, as " B." says, to " encourage him to lay up something," then it is the best for the native-born citizen, and Rhode Island should not tolerate a constitution that discriminates in favor of the foreigner to the detriment of the native. Should not the native-born citizen be " encouraged to lay up something?" Call the constitutional convention, give him the $134 clause and " encourage" him, and the next election will witness more than one-half the native voters disfranchised.

" B." tells us that the " possession of land has always been deemed the surest guaranty of the fidelity and loyalty of the citizen; having something to hold them to the soil, they have a direct interest in the maintenance of good government." Of course he means it works that way in Rhode Island, for we all know that the possession of land had no such effect on the fidelity or loyalty of our Southern brethren during " the late unpleasantness."

In 1846 my parents emigrated to the United States. Being only three years old, my consent was not asked nor my wishes consulted. When I arrived at the years of understanding—knowing nothing experimentally of the land of my fathers—I was glad of the change, and said " this people shall be my people, their God my God; where they die I will die, and there will I be buried." At the breaking out of the rebellion my father, as a Union soldier, laid down his life on the lower Mississippi. I entered the Union service in September, 1861, took my military degree at Roanoke Island under our own Burnside, and completed my course at Appomattox Court House in 1865—four years of active duty and not a day in the hospital. Is the possession of $134 worth of sand and gravel a better " guarantee of loyalty and fidelity " than the above record?

I am not alone; others went to the front in the hour of danger and remained there until they were no longer needed. We feel that we are entitled to some consideration. Has any native-born citizen done more to preserve the government that we all enjoy? Ought not the men who saved the government to have a voice in its management? Those who sought to destroy it have been for years making the laws under which we live, should not we have as many political privileges as they? It is not $134 worth of real estate that we object to, but we object to being subjected to restrictions not imposed on those who are no better as men, no more loyal as citizens, and have not the welfare of the nation any more at heart than we.

This is not a question of party; it is whether Rhode Island will rise superior to the prejudice that binds her, and do justice to the men who risked all in her defence. I am not a Democrat. I am not trying to make Democratic voters. I do not believe in the party, nor its principles, for I have been identified with the Republican party from the hour of its birth to the present time. I gave up politics, so far as voting is concerned, some four years since, because I knew that if I should be so unfortunate as to lose the real estate which entitled me to vote, I would stand on the same level, politically, as the man just landed on our shores; and I scorn to avail myself longer of a right of which, through misfortune, I might be so easily deprived.

I hear voices all around me saying if you do not like our restrictions you are at liberty to leave, and the senior Senator of Rhode Island, in the national Senate Chamber echoes: "They came here uninvited, and on their departure there is no restraint." Will the honorable Senator stand up in his place and tell us who "invited" the foreigners that emigrated in the Mayflower? Who gave the exclusive right of emigration to the foreigners who came here in the early part of the seventeenth century, and withholds it from those who came in the latter half of the nineteenth? Who "invited" Roger Williams to come to Rhode Island when the Pilgrims banished him from Massachusetts?

Where do the children of the foreigners who came here yesterday get the right to tell us we should not come to-day? We deny the assertion that on our "departure there is no restraint." Many of us have been here all our lives; we have intermarried with your sons and daughters; here our children were born, and the graves of our kindred dot the hillsides, while their dust is mingling with the soil, and yet we are told that "on our departure there is no restraint!" The God who directed the May-flower and led Roger Williams, gave them a charter of rights broader and deeper than any ever issued under the seal of the English government, and he has given to us a charter just as broad and just as deep. He has led us here, and, like the Union soldiers in the South during the war, we have come prepared to stay. While we stay we will be peaceable, law-abiding citizens, working for the best interests of our State, and trust that those who have the power in their hands may be led to let their better judgment prevail, and do us justice before it is too late.

The following communication to the Providence Journal of March 26, 1881, was from the pen of Dr. WILLIAM F. CHANNING, of Providence:

TAXATION AND REPRESENTATION SHOULD GO TOGETHER.

To the Editor of the Journal:

"Equality before the law" has been a watchword of free institutions. Equality of representation is the cardinal principle of a republican form of government. That taxation and representation should go together is an American axiom. A disfranchised people, in the historical order of things, are unequally taxed and inequitably governed.

The city of Providence is just now reaping the fruit of the unrepublican inequality of its representation. The rotten borough system of representation could not go much farther than that which prevails in Rhode Island, not by any choice the people ever made, but by a bad inheritance from the King Charles charter. The city of Providence, with nearly two-fifths of the population of the State, is arbitrarily assigned only one-sixth of the representation in the popular branch of the General Assembly, and only one thirty-sixth of the representation in the Senate. This outrage on the principle of popular self-government would be no greater, and hardly more glaring, if to the smallest town in the State were to be given nine-tenths of the whole of the so-called representation in the General Assembly; and if this principle of inequality might give the government of the State to the smallest town in it, why not to one family in that town, or to one man in that family in perpetuity, with no chance for the people ever to acquire the right of representation? How far would it be necessary to go in violating the principle of equal representation to justify a decision of the Supreme Court of the United States that our government is not republican?

While equality of popular representation in the popular branch of the Legislature is an essential of our American system, a corporate or municipal representation, within certain limits as to equality of population, has been tolerated in the Senate of the United States and in the Senate of some of the States. There would probably be no objection if Providence had its equal representation in the House of Representatives, to accept a representation in the Senate, enlarged from thirty-six to forty-five members, of one Senator for each ward of the city, instead of one Senator for the whole city, as at present. The wards of a city are the corporate bodies most nearly comparable with the towns in population.

It has been objected, with some show of justice, to the equal representation of cities, that the concentration of votes gave added political power. For this reason, when the constitution of Massachusetts was amended and Boston applied for equal representation, the representation was granted, but it was provided that each ward should elect its own representatives, instead of the election of representatives on a general ticket by the whole city, as previously practiced in Boston, and now in Providence. This division of political power is on every account just and desirable. It is a brake applied to that dangerous element in American politics, the "machine."

It may be asked how is the city of Providence to obtain its equal representation in the State government, except by appeal to the Supreme Court of the United States. Would a rotten borough constitutional convention dispossess a rotten borough legislature? Or shall, for the first time in its history, the people of the State be represented in a constitutional conven-

tion in proportion to the sovereignty of numbers? And if so, how shall
such a convention be called? Is or is not the power of initiating self-government inherent in the American people?

A VOTER UNDER THE KING CHARLES CHARTER.

At the regular meeting of the Equal Rights Association, on
the first Tuesday in March, 1881, Edwin Metcalf, Esq., who had
been unable to attend the hearings of the committee, gave an
address of absorbing interest, of which the following is a
synopsis:

HON. EDWIN METCALF, OF PROVIDENCE.

He began his remarks by saying that he had not made any special pre-
paration for what he should have to say, but having been in at the birth
of the instrument under which our State is now governed, he was pretty
familiar with the subject. He was sorry that he had not attended the recent discussions, but thought there was scarcely anything new to be said
on the subject. He started life under the system that prevailed before the
present constitution was adopted. Under this system, he, as the oldest
son of a real estate owner in this city, had the right of suffrage, which
even his brothers, when they became of age, did not possess. The absurdity and injustice of that system struck him even at that time. It was
a rotten plank in a rotten system, and yet that was one of the enormities
that helped along the suffrage movement that resulted in the "People's
Constitution." He would, however, affirm that the old charter of Rhode
Island was a great deal better to live under than the constitution which
was subsequently adopted. The principal objection to the old charter was
its peculiar system of representation to the General Assembly. Newport
was given six Representatives; Providence, Warwick and Portsmouth
four each, and the other towns of the State two each. The system was
established in the reign of King Charles, when Newport was the chief
town of the colony, and was undoubtedly good enough for the condition
of things at that time. The old charter, however, could have been
changed at any time by a vote of the General Assembly. Of course to
the people of Newport such an act would have been a harrowing up of
the souls of the righteous; but then the wishes of the rest of the State
might have been effectually carried out. The people, indeed, made a
mistake when they made up their minds to throw that whole machinery
overboard, and start with a new contrivance. What they have got now
is an institution that leads to greater and greater injustice as time ad-
vances. Col. Metcalf then criticised with considerable sarcasm the "sand
and gravel" system of suffrage, and asserted that it had been productive
of much political corruption. He said it would be a funny thing for a

man to hunt up among the various town records of the State the practically bogus deeds that were scattered round in former years in order to make voters. This system has always inculcated the idea that sand and gravel are more valuable than men. In fact, the present constitution is founded on prejudice, which has got to be rooted out before any improvement can come. Until within a few years the population of Rhode Island was of a very homogeneous character. The people in those days'didn't go abroad or imbibe the foolish political notions of other States. They believed in themselves and their peculiar local institutions. They considered themselves the purest patriots on the face of the earth. The Providence Journal, which stands by the present system, has been for many years a very able paper. Some of us when we get mad may try to assail it, but have to acknowledge that it carries a great many guns. Mr. Henry B. Anthony grew up in Kent County, a true native of the soil, and what Henry B. Anthony doesn't know about the prejudices of the countrymen of Rhode Island isn't worth knowing. [Laughter.] And what he doesn't know his associate from just over the Connecticut line can easily supply. The Journal is a Rhode Island institution, and when it sits down upon a man he feels the weight of the whole State of Rhode Island. [Laughter.] "We are going to govern Rhode Island in our own way, and you may help it if you can." That is the position the supporters of the present constitution have taken; that was the argument that was recently heard in the Senate of the United States. It isn't much of an argument, but it carries the vote of the State of Rhode Island.

The speaker next devoted his attention to the unequal system of representation under the present constitution. Providence has been steadily growing away from its representation. The city has no greater representation to-day than when it had a population of 40,000. This unequal representation was, in the opinion of the speaker, the greatest evil of the present constitution. It was a fundamental wrong that went right to the root of things. The property qualification was another great wrong and inconsistency. The speaker particularly denounced those old Jeffersonian Democrats who, with such deliberation and apparent pleasure, walk up to the polls whenever the question of a change in the constitution comes up, and deposit their ballots against the measure. Objection was also found to the system of appointing and maintaining the judiciary of the State.

Col. Metcalf took a retrospective view of the Dorr rebellion, and said that if Thomas W. Dorr had been as good a practical leader as he was a political theorist, he might have carried his points; especially would this have been true if some of the knowing ones in the State could have whispered in the ear of President Tyler that to sustain Mr. Dorr would put the Democratic party on a firm and lasting foundation in this State. The speaker further discussed the subject in its various bearings, and closed by expressing the belief that the people of Rhode Island would outgrow the present system sooner or later.

The following squibs, which appeared in the public press, are given as a contribution to the humor of the agitation. The first, which bears the date of January 24, 1881, was called out by the unexpected position taken by two members of the Judiciary Committee, that the General Assembly has no power to call a constitutional convention:

A LAMENT.

BY ONE OF THE PETITIONERS.

Alas! what a pity our fathers didn't mention,
That we boys, if very good, could hold a convention.
They never said we shouldn't, but didn't say we might,
" Ergo," cry the sages, "you haven't got the right."
'Twas very bad, indeed, their permission to deny,
But infinitely worse at once to up and die;
For thus they turned the lock and flung away the key,
And Rhode Island's " in a box" for all eternitee.

Soon after the great effort of Hon. H. B. Anthony, upon the floor of the United States Senate, and in consequence of the misleading figures which the speech contained, appeared the following *jeu d'esprit*:

THE "DEFENSE OF RHODE ISLAND."

(*Votes, 29,000 ; men, 77,000.*)

Henry B., (a Senator he,
Knowing his grammar to a T,
"*Present,* I am; *Future,* to be,")
Rather than see the suffrage made free,
Tortured arithmetic into the plea,
" Two in Rhode Island is greater than three!"

8

THE sentiments expressed by the various contributors to this pamphlet require, in closing, but little comment. To the people of other States the arguments here adduced will seem like attempting to prove an axiom; for, except in Rhode Island, the spirit of " Know-nothingism " is dead, the sovereignty of the people unquestioned. Nor in this State have her peculiar and un-American political institutions been supported by appeals to reason; they rest solely upon prejudice and a spirit of caste.

The movement for equal rights has not ceased. At this writing, July, 1881, open-air meetings are being held in the manufacturing villages situated northward of the city of Providence. Whether at an early period the suffrage in Rhode Island is to be made similar to that of other States rests wholly with her own people. It needs but a determined effort on the part of those who are wronged, and their sympathizers, to insure a speedy success. The trend of events in this country is and ever has been in the direction of greater freedom. Injustice and illiberality have proved temporary, while liberty and right are eternal.

CONSTITUTION AND OFFICERS

OF THE

EQUAL RIGHTS ASSOCIATION.

CONSTITUTION.

ARTICLE I. *Name.*—Equal Rights Association.

ART. II. *Object.*—This Association is formed as an aid to acquiring and maintaining in Rhode Island a government by the people. Therefore, its aim shall be—

(1) To extend and equalize the suffrage;

(2.) To disseminate political information;

(3.) To secure a full, free, and intelligent ballot;

(4.) To ignore national parties in State affairs;

(5.) To support for State officers such candidates only as are faithful to the fundamental principle, that the people of Rhode Island shall rule Rhode Island.

ART. III. *Membership.*—Any resident of Rhode Island, not less than twenty years of age, may become a member of this Association by paying the admission fee of one dollar and assenting to the Constitution.

ART. IV. *Officers.*—The officers of the Association shall be a President, five or more Vice-Presidents, a Treasurer, a Secretary, a Corresponding Secretary, and an Executive Committee of nine, all to be chosen annually at the first regular meeting in October.

ART. V. *Amendments.*—Amendments proposed to this Constitution shall lie upon the table until the next meeting.

☞ Public meetings are held on the first Tuesday evening of every month, excepting June, July and August, at Franklin Lyceum Hall, 62 Westminster street, Providence, R. I.

OFFICERS.

President,

Dr. L. F. C. GARVIN....................................Lonsdale.

Vice-Presidents,

WILLIAM VON GOTTSCHALCK, M. D...... ....Providence.
Hon. GEORGE L. CLARKE..............................Providence.
Mr. WALTER CALLENDER..............................Providence.
Mr. JOHN D'ARCY......................................Apponaug.
Mr. JOHN B. MARSH ....Central Falls.

Treasurer,

WILLIAM B. AVERY ....49 Exchange Place, Providence.

Secretary,

C. C. HEINTZEMAN......................176 Broad Street, Providence.

Corresponding Secretary,

HENRY APPLETON............... ....150 Transit Street, Providence.

Executive Committee.

CHARLES P. ADAMS....................................Pawtucket.
P. J. McCARTHY.......................................Providence.
JOHN B. MARSH.... ....Central Falls.
D. D. DONOVAN.......................................Providence.
HENRY APPLETON................... ....Providence.
CHARLES E. GORMAN..................................Providence.
LOUIS KRANZ ....Providence.
JAMES J. SULLIVAN....................................Central Falls.
JAMES H. LEWIS..................... ....Lonsdale.

www.ingramcontent.com/pod-product-compliance
Lightning Source LLC
Chambersburg PA
CBHW021633270326
41931CB00008B/997